This publication is dedicated
to the preservation of the
heritage of Canada's native peoples

Canada's Native Peoples

Editor
CHARLES J. HUMBER

Volume II
CANADA
HEIRLOOM SERIES

CANADA's Native Peoples

CANADA Heirloom Series, Volume II

Heirloom Publishing Inc., 2233 Argentia Road, Suite 304, Mississauga, ON L5N 2X7

PRESIDENT
Angela Dea Cappelli Clark

EDITOR-IN-CHIEF
Charles J. Humber

MANAGEMENT CONSULTANTS
William Melbourne & Associates

RESEARCH, EDITORIAL AND SUPPORT STAFF
Gil Baker, Leytha Miles Cobham, Reg Dawe,
Helen de Verteuil, Patricia Eden, Sharlene Hesselink,
Gordon Holmes, Patricia Korn, Lynn Pereira,
Helen Vanschoonhoven, Claudia Willetts

DESIGN
RK Graphic Communications
Amstier Graphics

COVER DESIGN
Hart Broudy, William Melbourne & Associates

PRINTER
St. Joseph Printing

COLOUR SEPARATIONS
Photra Limited

CANADA's *Native Peoples*
CANADA Heirloom Series, Volume II
Typeset, Printed and Bound in Canada
Copyright © 1988 by Heirloom Publishing Inc.

CANADIAN CATALOGUING IN PUBLICATION DATA

Main entry under title:

CANADA's Native Peoples

(CANADA Heirloom Series , v. II)
Includes index.
ISBN 0-9692182-4-9. — ISBN 0-9692182-6-5 (set).

1. Indians of North America — Canada. 2. Inuit — Canada.* 3. Métis — Canada.* I. Humber, Charles J. II. Series.

E78.C2C36 1988   971'.00497   C86-094385-2

Table of Contents

Contributors

EDITOR

CHARLES J. HUMBER, M.A. (Univ. of Wisconsin)
Born, Montreal, P.Q.; President, The John W. Fisher
Society; Director, The John Graves Simcoe Association;
President, The U.E.L. Assoc. of Canada (1982-84);
Secondary School teacher since 1969, Toronto Board of
Education; Co-editor, *LOYAL SHE REMAINS: A Pictorial
History of Ontario* (1984); Editor, *CANADA: From Sea
Unto Sea* (1986); Well-known collector of Canadiana

PETER CHRISTMAS, B.A. (St. Francis Xavier
Univ.), B.Ed. (Saint Mary's Univ.)
A Micmac from Sydney, Nova Scotia; Executive Direc-
tor, Micmac Association of Cultural Studies since 1973;
Executive Director, Union of Nova Scotia Indians,
1971-73; Vice-Principal/Teacher, Queens County, Nova
Scotia, 1962-71

IAN CREERY
Born, Ottawa; Canadian anthropologist, author, radio
and TV broadcaster specializing in Inuit concerns;
Worked with Inuit at Frobisher Bay and Broughton
Island, N.W.T., and as Fieldwork Co-ordinator for the
Inuit Tapirisat of Canada Land Claims Project; Fluent
in Inuktitut

IAN GETTY, M.A. (Univ. of Calgary)
Born, Tekkali, South India; Research Director, Nakoda
Institute, Stoney Tribal Administration, Alberta; Ph.D.
candidate (McMaster Univ.); Social Anthropologist; A
consultant in Constitutional discussions relating to
Indian issues. Co-edited *As Long as the Sun Shines and
Water Flows* with Antoine Lussier (1983)

WAYNE GETTY, M.A., M.S.W. (Univ. of Calgary)
Born, Coonoor, South India; Social Anthropologist;
Yorkton, Saskatchewan District Superintendant of Social
Development, Dept. of Indian and Northern Affairs;
Papers presented to The Berger Commission on the
Mackenzie Pipeline, the Lysik Inquiry on the Alaska
Highway Pipeline, the Alberta Environment Commis-
sion; Consultant, Stoney Indian Tribal Administration,
1972-75; Community Development Consultant, Indian
Association of Alberta, 1970-72; Since 1976, Consultant,
Indian Rights for Indian Women

TOM HILL
Born, Ohsweken, Ontario; A Seneca; Director, Wood-
land Indian Cultural and Educational Centre (Brant-
ford, Ontario); With Dept. of Indian Affairs and
Northern Development for eight years; Organized
exhibitions of Indian Art in Brazil, Japan and Europe;
Co-author *Norval Morrisseau and the Emergence of the
Image Makers* (1984)

ANTOINE LUSSIER, M.Ed. (Univ. of Manitoba)
A Metis from Saskatchewan; Ph.D. candidate (Univ. of
Manitoba); Dean, Post Secondary and Applied Studies,
Keewatin Community College, The Pas, Manitoba;
Author of numerous publications including *The Metis:
Canada's Forgotten People* (1975); Broadcaster: "Our
Native Land", CBC, Manitoba Region (1969-71);
Research Consultant, Manitoba Metis Federation;
Co-edited *As Long as the Sun Shines and Water Flows*
with Ian Getty (1983)

ELIZABETH McLUHAN, M.A., (Univ. of N.M.)
Director Curator, Art Gallery of York University;
Former Curator, Thunder Bay National Exhibition
Centre and Centre for Indian Art; Native Arts Consul-
tant, Government of Ontario, 1974-81; Co-author, *Norval
Morrisseau and the Emergence of the Image Makers* (1984);
Organizer of numerous exhibitions and corresponding
catalogues including *Altered Egos: The Multi-Media Work
of Carl Beam* (1984); *Daphne Odjig: A Retrospective 1984-
1985;* Daughter of the late Marshall McLuhan

JOAN RYAN, Ph.D. (Univ. of British Columbia)
Born, Montreal, P.Q.; Professor of Anthropology, Uni-
versity of Calgary; Author, *Wall of Words* (1978); Editor,
Alaskan Native Secondary School Drop-Outs (1962);
Researcher, Stoney Cultural Programme Curriculum
Research and Nakoda Institute Research on Indian
Self-Government

CAROL SHEEHAN, M.A.
(Univ. of British Columbia)
Ph.D. candidate (Univ. of Toronto); Project Director
for U.B.C. Museum of Anthropology (1975); Editor,
Publications, Canadian Conservation Institute, Nation-
al Museums of Canada, Ottawa (1978-79); Assistant
Curator of Ethnology, Glenbow Museum (1979-82);
Presently teaching Canadian Native Art and Culture
at the Univ. of Calgary

Foreword

The aboriginal peoples of Canada have long suffered indignities, both from a lack of recognition of their contributions to our heritage, culture and social structure, and from limitations imposed upon them that have inhibited their development.

CANADA's Native Peoples helps provide that recognition as well as an impetus for the private sector to work together with native people for a future of great promise, not only for native people themselves but for the benefit and enhancement of all Canadians. It is a responsibility and a challenge....

Murray B. Koffler, C.M.
Founding Chairman,
Canadian Council for Native Business

Even those of us who were brought up Christian on the Six Nations lands knew about the Three Sisters. We may not have known the details of their legend — we suspected that kids who were brought up in the Longhouse religion got that gift — but it was clear to see how the Corn, the Beans and the Squash, when planted together, enabled each other's growth and certainly complemented each other's beauty.

It is with a similar understanding of what we might call Canada's Three Sisters, her History, Heritage and Culture, that we at the Association for Native Development in the Performing and Visual Arts support the publication of *CANADA's Native Peoples.*

We work on a day to day basis for the development of contemporary Native arts in many of Canada's original cultures, with many Native artists, and we have learned that no culture can grow unless the soil of its heritage is cared for and the roots of its history are maintained. Uprooting, transplanting, slash and burn, are less than wise farming.

We think *CANADA's Native Peoples* will be a tool of great use in the tilling of Canada's cultural soil and the tending of her cultural roots. We can expect flowers and fruit as beautiful as the Corn, the Beans and the Squash.

Daniel David Moses
President
Association for Native Development in the Performing and Visual Arts

"The Dance of Life" was painted by ANDPVA Board member, Maxine Noel, who signs her work in her native Sioux language, Ioyan Mani, "She Who Walks Beyond".

Introduction

"The history of Canada's Indians is a chronicle of the white man's disinterest."   Harold Cardinal, 1969.

The first threads in the fabric of Canada's culture, heritage and history were woven by her native peoples.

We at Heirloom Publishing Inc., publishers of *CANADA: From Sea Unto Sea*, have produced *CANADA's Native Peoples* as Volume II of the *CANADA Heirloom Series* to help give the distinctive recognition our first nations deserve.

The work of nine knowledgeable Canadians, three of whom are members of our first nations, has been skillfully orchestrated by our editor, Charles J. Humber, with a dedication and passion for Canada that has been an inspiration to all throughout the development of the series.

We extend our thanks to Murray Koffler, Founding Chairman of *The Canadian Council for Native Business* and to the *Association for Native Development in the Performing and Visual Arts* for their assistance and dedication. The support of the *Government of Ontario* through the *Ministry of Culture and Communications,* the Honourable Lily Munro, Minister, is also gratefully acknowledged.

While this volume sympathizes with the above quotation, it responds as well to Chief Crowfoot's observations of 1890.

> "[Life] is a flash of a firefly in the night. It is the breath of the buffalo in wintertime. It is the shadow that runs across the grass and loses itself in the sunset."

This slender volume undoubtedly does more than capture a "flash", a "breath" and a "shadow". It records the legacy of Canada's first peoples for generations to come....

Angela Dea Cappelli Clark

Angela Dea Cappelli Clark
President

Canada 12
Inuit - Hunting
Les Inuits - La chasse

Indians of the Subarctic / Les Indiens du Nord — Canada 8

Canada 8
Indians of the Pacific Coast / Les Indiens de la Côte du Pacifique

Canada 8
Indians of the Plains / Les Indiens des Plaines

Canada 6
Louis Riel

Canada's Native Peoples

The Algonkians / Les Algonquins
Canada 8

The Iroquoians / Les Iroquoiens
Canada 10

Paul Kane painter / peintre
Canada 7

OVERLEAF: Stamps Reproduced Courtesy the Canada Post Corporation.

Stamp: *Algonkian Artifacts. The Micmacs, a large group of Algonkians in Canada's maritime provinces, are a resourceful people whose artifacts today are highly prized by collectors worldwide.* [*Canada Post Corporation*]

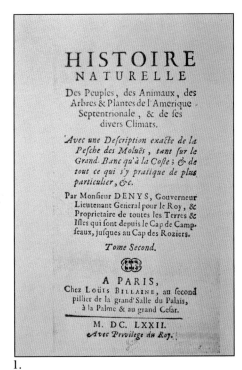

1.

1. *Title page of N. Denys' "Histoire Naturelle" published in 1672.* [*Courtesy National Library Collection*] 2. *"Domiciliated Indians of North America", by G. Heriot, ca. 1807.* [*Public Archives of Canada* [*PAC*]/*C-12781*].

Micmac Aboriginal Life
Peter Christmas

With the Beothuks and Inuit, the Micmacs share whatever distinction there is in having been the first to be "discovered by the Europeans." For the Micmac, the contact apparently began with the exploration of Cape Breton by French Bretons in the early 1500s.

At this time the Micmacs had their own territory, a civilization with a distinct system of government, education and economy. The Micmacs divided their territory into districts. The seven districts were as follows:

2.

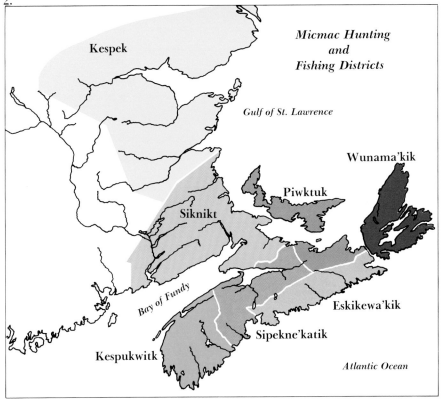

Wunama'kik, now Cape Breton Island;

Piwktuk (where gaseous explosions erupt), represented by the areas of Pictou and Prince Edward Island;

Eskikewa'kik (skin dressers' territory), stretching from Guysborough to Halifax counties;

Sipekne'katik (ground nut place), extending over the counties of Halifax, Lunenburg, Kings, Hants and Colchester;

Kespukwitk, covering the counties of Queens, Shelburne, Yarmouth, Digby and Annapolis;

Siknikt, including Cumberland and the New Brunswick counties of Westmoreland, Albert, Kent, St. John, Kings and Queens; and

Kespek (the last land), a district north of the Richibucto, its allied rivers and parts of Gaspé not occupied by the Iroquois (Kwetejk).

Micmac government was organized around three main types of Chief: the Local Chief, the District Chief, and the Grand Chief.

The Local Chief looked after the immediate affairs of the summer village inhabitants of the District. He presided over the "Council of Elders," the governing body of that village. Family heads or representatives made up the council of elders. The Local Chief provided dogs for the chase, canoes for transportation, provisions for hunting expeditions and emergency food supplies in times of need.

Each of the seven Micmac Districts had a Chief (*sagamaw*) who, like all Chiefs, was usually the eldest son of some powerful family group. He received much of his power from the size of his family. To maintain a large family, the Chief took several wives. There appeared to be no jealousy among them because it was considered an honour to be a Chief's wife.

The District Chief presided over the Council of Local Chiefs within his domain. The Council usually met in spring or autumn to resolve such issues as peace and war. Decisions in the council were reached by consensus. Young men who had not yet killed their first moose, and women and children, had no say.

When the Micmac wished to deal with issues affecting the whole nation, a Grand Council consisting of all District Chiefs and their families would be convened by a Grand Chief who was a District Chief designated by the Grand Council to be its chief spokesman.

Besides assigning hunting and fishing territories to the Chiefs and their families, the Grand Council ratified treaties of friendship with other tribes and later with the colonial government of Nova Scotia.

Unlike European monarchs, a good chief deliberately humbled himself in dress and lifestyle to show that the well-being of his own people came first. He also shared his food with the poor, even with those in the nearby villages. When he and his family paid the usual

Comtemporary dress of a Micmac chief.
[Micmac Association of Cultural Studies [MACS]]

summer visits, gifts of meats and fruit were usually taken along. His generosity was not supported by taxing the people. No one in the village had to provide him with food or furs. Because he was the best hunter, he could easily obtain these necessities.

Conservation was a major concern of the aboriginal tribal governments. In the Micmac land, game was not always plentiful. Heavy snowfalls and extremely cold temperatures reduced the number of moose, a major source of winter food supply. Floods, hurricanes, droughts and lightning storms, which caused forest fires, could easily disturb the delicate balance of nature. Any major break in the food chain meant starvation for both the Micmac and his brothers, the animals. As a result, the Council of Chiefs assigned separate hunting and fishing districts and passed tribal laws in order to control hunting at different seasons.

The purpose of the Micmac educational system was not at all different from the purpose of education today—to teach the skills necessary for a full and a rewarding life. The skills required then were quite different from today's. A youth needed to know how to make various implements such as bows, arrows, lances, shields, fish-

1. *Shellfish clamp typical of Micmac culture.* 2. *Micmacs drying cod prior to smoking process.* 3. *Micmac women dressing moose.* [*MACS*] 4. *"Micmac Encampment by a River", ca. 1800, unknown artist.* [*PAC/C-114481*]

1.

3.

2.

4.

traps and weirs, snowshoes, canoes, axes and knives. Woodlore was extremely important. Methods of hunting, fishing, trailblazing, and preparations of food, clothing and shelter were basic. It was even important to know how to tell time by observing natural events.

Children were taught according to their future roles. The tasks of the individuals within the Micmac tribe were determined by sex. Men did the hunting and made the bows, arrows, lances, shields, fish-traps and weirs, snowshoe frames and canoes. They also manufactured the cradleboards and all other articles of wood, even the tobacco pipe. Women carried game back to the camp, transported all the camp equipment, prepared and preserved the food, crafted birchbark dishes, boxes and baskets, often with porcupine quill, wove mats from rushes, made robes of goose feathers, made stockings and moccasins, corded the snowshoes, moved and set up the wigwams, fetched the water and took care of the children.

Micmacs took pride in their bows which they made from an unsplit piece of maple. They were first roughly shaped with a stone axe (*tmi'kn*) and a knife (*wagan*). For a finer finish and polish, oyster shells were used. Arrows were made of cedar. Cedar has the

1. Micmac birch and cedar canoes showing elevated gun-wale. [MACS] 2. Examples of serving baskets (early 20th century) made from ash split and stripped by crooked knife. [MACS] 3. Micmac quillwork boxes by Christina Morris, ca. 1804-1886. [MACS] 4. "Micmac Woman". Water colour by Mary R. McKie, ca. 1850. [PAC/C-9563] 5. Traditional Micmac basket-weaving, P.E.I., ca. 1900 [Robert Wilson] 6. Micmac quillwork chair back. [Royal Ontario Museum, Toronto]

1.

2.

3.

4.

5.

6.

quality of splitting straight and being light. At first, bones were used for the tip, but later iron replaced them. Eagle tail feathers were prized for guiding the arrows.

In canoe making, the Micmac sought the largest birch trees from which to obtain bark for an 18 to 24 foot canoe which was about two feet wide in the middle. Micmacs used the brightness of the firefly as the sign when the bark would be the easiest to remove. Cedar slats were used for the inside lining and for the ribs. The thread to sew the canoe came from fir roots. For waterproofing, the Micmac used fir gum which had been chewed daily by the women and girls. The paddles were of beech. One of the important features of the Micmac canoe was the elevated gunwale which prevented waves from splashing inward.

Jesuit missionaries described the snowshoe as a "broad piece of network." Micmacs called it "*agam*," indicating that the aboriginal snowshoe may have been made from white ash (*agamog*). Later beech was used.

Men worked the thick wooden strips into oval frames which measured waist high. The curved ends were then bound together with leather made from dressed moose skins. For central support, two slats of wood were fastened about two hands apart across each frame.

Women corded the three parts—toe, central support and heel—in a criss-cross and a diagonal fashion. The design enabled a hunter to walk in a deep, soft snow. For durability, thicker strips of leather were used to fill the central support. An opening in front of the central support accommodated the toe of the moccasin. In this way a hunter was able to walk rhythmically without lifting the heel of the snowshoe.

The Micmac snowshoe may not have been built for speed, but it proved very formidable against snowbound game such as the caribou and the moose.

Micmac medicine and first-aid practices relied on plants and animals. Occasionally youth were instructed in the medicinal values of each plant and animal. This medicine could be very effective. Cartier credits an Indian brew made from alder bark with saving his crew from scurvy.

Micmacs not only used herbs for minor illnesses such as head colds, coughs and stomach disorders, but also practiced blood-letting, applied poultices, and used emetics.

The emetics induced vomiting and were made from roots of various milkweeds, seeds of leather wood and black alder. For any swelling or boils, several incisions were made to draw out the blood. For an open wound, the favourite remedy was the application of a

Types of snowshoes used by East Coast Indians, including Micmacs in 18th, 19th and 20th centuries.

slice of beaver's kidney to absorb blood and pus. A poultice made from fir balsam was used to dress the wound.

One of the most important medical practices was the use of the sweat lodge. The lodge consisted of a wigwam frame which was completely covered with birch bark and skins; a shallow pit in the centre of the lodge held the red-hot, fire-heated stones. Eight or more men sat naked around the pit for an hour or so, chanting, recounting legends and meditating. Periodically, they poured water on the hot stones. At the end of the ritual, each man dashed into a nearby lake or river or rolled in the snow, then dressed and retired to his wigwam, refreshed both physically and spiritually.

Dependence upon the sea and its products was high in the Micmac world, for it supplied about 90 percent of his food. One method of fishing relied on weirs. These weirs, consisting of stakes driven side by side, were placed almost erect and supported by wooden logs with only enough space for the fish to enter. Sometimes rocks were used for more support. The latter structure was first observed by the crew of the *Marigold* at the northern tip of Cape Breton Island in 1593.

1.

1. *Sweat lodges were used by Micmac men for physical and spiritual revitalization.* [MACS] 2. *Examples of contemporary Micmac fish spears.* [MACS] 3. *Contemporary Micmac eel weir.* [MACS] 4. *Close-up of Micmac fish spears.* [MACS]

3.

4.

2.

For the spawning runs, the Micmac relied upon fishtraps. First, slats measuring about 1.5 m long and 5 cm wide were obtained by splitting fir limbs in two. One of these slats was formed into a hoop about 37 cm across. The hoop formed the middle part of the trap. Each slat was carefully tied to the hoop with birch bark strips. At one end a wigwam shaped birch bark was placed inward so that the eels could enter and not escape. The other end was closed just enough to let the undersized eels pass through.

For large fish like the sturgeon and the salmon (*plamu*), the Micmacs used the harpoon which consisted of a wooden staff, a

Mastering the bow and arrow. [MACS]

pointed bone at one end and a line at the other so that the harpoon could be attached to the canoe. At night, torches of birch were used to attract the sturgeon. Once it started to circle the canoe, the fisherman would harpoon it. The sturgeon would then swim with great fury, dragging the canoe, until it became exhausted. This method of fishing, known as *sagsikwemk,* is still being carried on today.

Since fish were extremely plentiful, hunting for game required more skill than did fishing. Consequently, good moose hunters were held in high esteem. The Micmac hunter had to master skillful ways of hunting moose (*tia'm*). One such way was tracking. Tracks and even the moose's dung indicated its sex and age. Having positioned themselves downwind from the moose, the hunters would stalk it until they got as close as 50 paces. At this distance, mastery with the bow ensured an eventual kill. In the winter, with the aid of snowshoes and the dogs, the moose was easy game because it was not as swift in the heavy snow. If the moose were in a herd, the Indians took advantage of the moose's habit of "yarding," that is, of following each other in single file along a widely circular path. One Indian would chase the herd along the "yard" while others would lie in ambush and spear each moose.

Micmacs' lives were shaped by their belief in a supernatural power which governed them and their land. Why did they have such reverence for the sun, the moon, the weather? Why didn't they waste any part of the game? Why did they share their food? After a great feast, why did they leave portions of food on the ground? Why wouldn't they feed bones to their dogs? Why were valued personal possessions buried with them? The answers to these questions are found in Micmac religion.

Micmacs believed in a Great Spirit, a Great Creator or a Great

The sun was considered by the Micmac as one of the most powerful of the mediator "pure" deities created by the Great Spirit. This view of the setting sun along the Nova Scotian coastline captures in a haunting way Micmac mysticism associated with this "deity". [Photo/Wayne Getty]

Mystery who created the universe, the supernatural and living things. This Great Spirit *kjiniskam* was invisible, non-natural and did not have a human form. He was capable of making his presence felt in the sun, the moon and the heavens. He controlled the destinies of all material and non-material things. He was all powerful and all present.

The Great Spirit created mediators: the "pure" deities and the "transformer" deities were more powerful than man. The most important of the "pure" deities were the sun, the earth, the moon, the four directions, the stars, the thunder, the weather and other phenomena. Of these, the sun and the moon were deemed the most powerful.

The "transformer" deities were capable of bestowing their supernatural powers on man. The most powerful and the most benevolent was the *mi'kmuesu* created by the Great Spirit. When the *mi'kmuesu* assumed human forms and quality, he still retained his enormous powers and immortality. Even though he lived in a land far away form the Micmacs, his presence was always felt.

It was the aboriginal belief that after death, the "free-soul" would travel to the land of the dead (land of the Souls). It was also believed that the "free-soul" could remain on earth to haunt the living. For this reason, after a great feast, Micmacs left portions of food for the souls which stalked the wigwams of their friends and relatives. In the Land of Souls (*wa'so'g*), both the souls of man and beast existed in harmony, and starvation was non-existent. The aboriginal Micmac believed that his free-soul could return to its former body and have its life-soul restored. In other words, when the departed soul returned, the body began to function as before. Anyone who returned from the dead was thought to possess strong supernatural powers.

In reincarnation, both the free-soul and the life-soul returned to a body recreated in some mystical way from the remains of former bodies. These remains were most often bones. Consequently in his aboriginal world there were many taboos associated with bones. Moose, beaver, caribou, bear and marten bones could not be burned or given to the dogs. If the remains were treated badly or left unused, the soul of the departed animal would convey this to the other animal souls in *wa'so'g*. For example, a reincarnated moose learning of this abuse would look upon the Micmac with disfavour and moose consequently would become scarce.

The Micmacs were among the first native peoples in North America converted to Christianity. On June 24, 1610, some five years after the establishment of the first permanent settlement in North America at Port Royal by Champlain, Grand Chief Membertou was baptized there, as were 20 members of his family, by Abbé Jessé Fleché.

Grand Chief Membertou, who lived at St. Mary's Bay or Annapolis Bay, was a famous *sagamaw*. All chiefs called *sagamaw* were said to possess a combination of supernatural powers such as *ginap* and *puoin*. A chief with *ginap* was considered very strong, able to pick up tremendous loads, bend guns, or even, as legend says, drink buckets of boiling grease. His fleeting powers were benevolent and timely. The *puoin*—wizard or witch—was the last descendant of the medicine man, possessing many of his powers such as predicting the future, conjuring up spirits to heal the sick and predicting game.

According to the Jesuit *Relations*, Chief Membertou was "impressed" to find good hunting after praying to the Christian God. Throughout the years of early Micmac Christianization, the powers of both *ginap* and *puoin* were challenged by the might of the new religion. The *sagamaw* healed by calling upon the mystical powers of the objects he carried in his leather pouch; the missionary did the same with the crucifix. The Jesuit *Relations* state that when Chief Membertou's son became ill, "We put upon the sufferer a bone taken from the precious relic of the glorified Saint Lawrence, Archbishop of Dublin in Ireland." He recovered and Christianity gained a firm hold. It's further reported that 140 Micmac were baptized by the Abbé Fleché after they saw him performing a ceremony with "mysterious signs and sounds of water."

In the French and English wars, the Micmacs sided with the

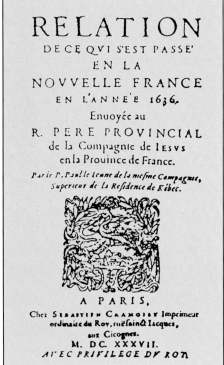

RELATION
DE CE QVI S'EST PASSE'
EN LA
NOVVELLE FRANCE
EN L'ANNE'E 1636.
Enuoyée au
R. PERE PROVINCIAL
de la Compagnie de IESVS
en la Prouince de France.
Par le P. Paulle Leune de la mefme Compagnie,
Superieur de la Refidence de Kébec.

A PARIS,
Chez SEBASTIEN CRAMOISY Imprimeur
ordinaire du Roy, rue fainct Iacques,
aux Cicognes.
M. DC. XXXVII.
AVEC PRIVILEGE DV ROY

1. *Church of the Most Holy Trinity, Indian Reserve, Whycocomagh, Cape Breton, ca. 1910. Micmacs were among the first native peoples in North America to convert to Christianity. [C.J. Humber]* 2. *Title page of one of the Jesuit "Relation[s]" published in 1637 recording the happenings in New France. [Hudson's Bay Company]*

French. Led by the French Missionary Abbé Le Loutre, they constantly harassed the English settlers. With the help of Abbé Pierre Maillard, who toiled with the Micmacs until his death in 1762, the British colonial government sought to end Micmac hostilities and the French influence by entering into "treaties of friendship." In return for the promise to "bury the hatchet," the Micmacs were guaranteed their basic rights to hunting, fishing and fowling territories. At no time did the Micmacs sign treaties surrendering their traditional use and occupancy of their aboriginal districts. The colonial and later the Nova Scotia government failed to honour these treaties.

Today the Micmacs are still struggling through their political associations to have their aboriginal rights honoured, respected and compensated. Their land claims must be commensurate with the loss of use and occupancy. They also must make it possible for Micmacs to achieve a better life. The constitutional talks with the Government of Canada and the provinces have yet to yield substantial results, but a significant Supreme Court decision handed down on November 21, 1985 upholding treaty rights in Nova Scotia will strengthen the bargaining position of all Micmacs in future talks with governments. The landmark ruling—a 7-0 decision—acquitted James Matthew Simon of charges, under the Nova Scotia legislation, of possessing a rifle and ammunition while travelling in deer country near the reserve in the 1980 closed hunting season. The decision is based on the wording of the 1752 Treaty signed between Chief Sachem of the Micmac tribe, Jean Baptiste Cope, and the then Governor of Nova Scotia, Peregrine Thomas Hopson, granting Micmacs "free liberty to hunt and fish as usual."

1. Micmac Grand Chief Donald Marshall and members of his council present the Nova Scotia Aboriginal Rights Paper to the Minister of Indian Affairs and Northern Development, Warren Allmand at the Eskasoni Reserve, 1976. [MACS] 2. As the European population expanded in Canada, the Micmac lost more and more of their land. This picture depicts a Micmac family overlooking Halifax Harbour from Dartmouth while Halifax expands. [PAC/C-102863] 3. "Micmac Indians", anonymous, oil on canvas, ca. 1850. [National Gallery of Canada /6663, Ottawa]

1.

2.

3.

The Indians of the St. Lawrence Lowlands
Tom Hill

Stamp: *A large percentage of native people living along the St. Lawrence lowlands are Iroquoian. A people close to nature, in the past, they celebrated the seasons with ritual false faces.* [*Canada Post Corporation*]

The history of man's arrival and occupation of the St. Lawrence Valley lowlands has been lost to time. The sciences have been able to give us some information about prehistoric life as artifacts are unearthed and new archaeological data are documented and proven.

The theory is that man most likely entered America some 50,000 years ago by crossing a land and ice bridge extending from present-day Siberia to Alaska. It was the age of the hairy mammoths, giant ground sloths, big horn bisons, great striped lions and giant beavers. Today this age faintly survives in oral folk-tales of some of the first North Americans. The prevailing view is that this migration was a gradual process with ensuing dispersals throughout North and South America. The exact connections between prehistoric and historic peoples of the St. Lawrence lowlands have yet to be determined.

When the first Europeans sailed up the St. Lawrence, they encountered aboriginal peoples belonging to two linguistic groups: the Algonkian and the Iroquoian. Today linguists, archaeologists and anthropologists theorize that the prehistoric Iroquoian are more recent arrivals in the region than the Algonkians, deducing that their migration north probably originated from the south. The Algonkians most likely gravitated south from the northern forests and tundra and settled along the St. Lawrence.

Both the Iroquoian and the Algonkian peoples had a cosmological structure or a world view designed to accommodate their concept of creation and their existence on earth. Generally, throughout North America, traditional native thought has rationalized the universe as a layered structure with the earth suspended between the celestial vault of the sky-world and the murky realm of the underworld, entered through the deepest lakes and rivers. The sky and the underworld were personified by a pair of mythic beings: a celestial bird or thunderbird and underwater panther or sea serpent. These beings constantly engaged in a life and death struggle, with man forced to act as mediator between these antithetical forces in order to preserve his health and well-being. Images of these two beings appeared on many objects from prehistoric times through to historic times. To the Algonkian peoples settling along the St. Lawrence, the total effect of the environment was so attuned to maintain a balance between physical and spiritual needs that the slightest change in this harmony would certainly summon, in some religious ritual, the powers of these two forces. Such an interconnection between the spiritual and physical world played a less significant role for the prehistoric Iroquoians who learned to respond

Corn Mask Serigraph by Minielle Sioui from Village Huron, Lorretteville, Quebec. Corn, beans and squash were the diet mainstays of lowland Indians. [*Woodland Indian Cultural Educational Centre* [*WICEC*]]

to their environment through agriculture and trade.

Although traces of the prehistoric concept that the universe is a layered structure are still evident in Iroquoian oral history, the Iroquoian creation story most likely evolved over the centuries to accommodate a constantly changing world. As agriculture dominated the early economies, it is understandable that the creation story would rationalize the Iroquoian's cultivation of corn, beans and squash.

Iroquois still believe that the creation process is both dynamic and ongoing and that man was placed on earth to create and recreate the good works of creation. The story is epic in proportions and

"The Creation Story", contemporary painting by Arnold Jacobs, showing Iroquoian interpretation of creation. This dramatic scene depicts a falling woman, heavy with child, being escorted to the back of the Great Turtle, master of all animals. See text on following page. [*WICEC*]

extremely complex. It would be a mistake to assume that the following synopsis of the creation story included all truths that have evolved over time in its retelling.

According to this synopsis people lived beyond the sky because deep waters covered the entire earth. Then a pregnant woman fell from the heavens towards the water. All the water animals such as the beaver, otter and muskrat viewed her fall as a reflection in the water and argued about whether she was coming up from the watery underworld. However, the ducks and geese believed she was falling from the sky and flew up to her, breaking her fall by overlapping their wings and protecting her from the terrors of the water. They carried her to the Great Turtle, master of all the animals, who volunteered his strong back as a plinth upon which to set the pregnant woman. First, however, he ordered the water animals to dive down to the bottom of the water and bring up some of the earth that also fell from the sky with the woman. When this magic earth had been recovered and placed upon his back, the Great Turtle began to grow into a large island. As the island increased in size, quakings of the earth were felt as the Great Turtle stretched and moved. Eventually, the woman gave birth to a daughter who in turn gave birth to twin sons. One twin who was born naturally was responsible for corn, fruit, tobacco and all good things that grow. The other twin, born through the armpit of the daughter, was responsible for weeds, vermin and other evils upon the earth.

The Iroquoians and the Algonkians who inhabited the St. Lawrence lowlands had strong tribal identities beyond the basic nuclear families. The Iroquoians lived in palisaded villages in long communal lodges. Their villages were stabilized by their agricultural pursuits whereas the Algonkians generally lived in dome-

1.

1. *"Birth of Good and Evil" (1982), Vincent Bombery (b. 1958). This steatite carving illustrates the Iroquoian legend of Mother Earth giving birth to the Primal Twins, representing good and evil. The good twin is Sky Holder; the evil one, Flint, bursting from his mother's armpit, is destined to become ruler of the underworld. [Collection of National Museum of Man, Ottawa. Photo/Helen Wilson]* 2. *Huron longhouse at Ste. Marie among the Hurons near Midland, Ontario during construction. [WICEC]*

2.

shaped individual bark wigwams more suited to a nomadic lifestyle dependent on hunting. Even today's Algonkians, such as the Montagnais and the Naskapi, have a system of hunting rights and conservation of game reflecting their ancient lifestyles. The Iroquoians and the Algonkians, as well, came to have confederacies of various tribes. The Algonkians created the Abnaki and Powhatan Confederacy while the Iroquoians created the Wyandot Confederacy, the Attiwandaronk or Neutral Confederacy and, last and most powerful, the Iroquois League of Five Nations.

Algonkian dome-shaped wigwam. [*WICEC*]

The League of the Ho-de-no-sau-nee, the Iroquois Confederacy, was composed of the Mohawk, Onondaga, Seneca, Oneida and the Cayuga and was believed to have been established sometime between 1400 A.D. and 1600. It was created primarily as a peacekeeping body which sought to negotiate from a position of power.

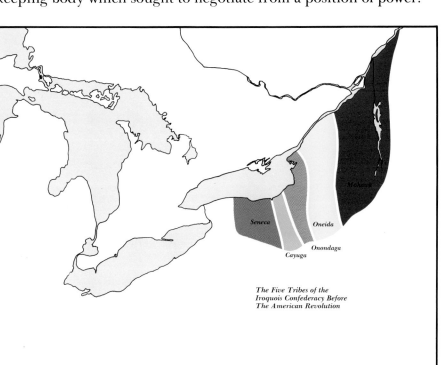

The Five Tribes of the Iroquois Confederacy Before The American Revolution

The Iroquois Confederacy is a political structure woven into the delicate fabric of the religion. Its principles and organization were derived from those of the religion and its power from the common ideology which was shared among member nations. Its practice spread to and included the people it was designed to serve and its politics was secure and accommodating.

When they first met Europeans, the Five Nations were already organized into the League of the Ho-de-no-sau-nee. Oral history says that this confederacy was accomplished by the semidivine heroes, Deganawidah, born of a virgin, and Hiawatha, his disciple. It should be noted that this Hiawatha is not the one immortalized in H.W. Longfellow's 1855 poem, "The Song of Hiawatha". Each

"Thadodaho", contemporary painting by Richard Hill. Thadodaho, an evil sorcerer, is here depicted with Hiawatha. According to legend, he was the last of the warrior chiefs to accept the peace offered by the semi-divine Deganawidah and his disciple Hiawatha. The wampum belt in the background symbolizes the pact. [WICEC]

of the Five Nations has a different tale describing how Deganawidah and Hiawatha visited each nation and gained acceptance for the establishment of peace among the warring nations.

Thadodaho (Atotarho), the powerful Onondaga chief, was the last to join. Oral history describes Thadodaho as an evil sorcerer. One translation of his name compares his head to a nest of writhing snakes and suggests his mind was confused with evil. Although the etymology is uncertain, another translation of Thadodaho's name is said to mean, "He whose house blocks the path". Regardless of the actual translation, his name does imply his reluctance to accept the great peace offered by Deganawidah and Hiawatha.

When he finally accepted and the Confederacy of Five Nations was established, special concessions were made to Thadodaho and the Onondagas. They held the chairmanship of the Council and became known as "first among equals." The Onondagas were given the highest number of chiefs, 14 in all, and the exclusive right to summon a meeting of all the council members. The Onondaga village became the capital of the Five Nations.

The judicial and executive powers of the Confederacy were invested in a body of 50 chiefs. Of these, 14 came from the Onondaga, nine from the Oneida, 10 from the Cayuga, eight from the Seneca and nine from the Mohawk. These 50 civil chiefs, separate from the warrior chiefs, were appointed whenever military undertakings were required and terminated once the military action was completed. The warrior chiefs' positions were not hereditary as in the case of the 50 civil chiefs.

Civil chiefs were appointed according to their respective clans.

As Iroquois clans are matrilineal, a new-born child received a name belonging to his mother's side. The perpetuation of certain personal names which also entailed certain roles in society was and is the responsibility and right of the clans.

When one of the civil chiefs' positions became vacant through death, the clan mother who in most cases was the most senior woman of the clan, would select the man who would assume the name and hence become the next chief. This selection was made in consultation with other women belonging to that clan. A woman delegate would then carry the news to chiefs of the clan belonging to the same "side" of the deceased chiefs' clan. They had the power to veto the clan mother's selection in which case another women's meeting was held to select a new candidate. Once approved by the clan chiefs, the candidate was presented to the Grand Council for ratification. A public ceremony was held and the chief was adorned with the honours of the deer, the symbol of his prestigious office. Also, if a chief proved unsatisfactory, the clan mother could remove him from his chiefmanship in a process called "dehorning" which involved the taking away of his metaphorical deer antlers.

Another group of chiefs, known as "Pine Tree Chiefs", held positions gained by merit rather than heredity. They occupied their honourary places on the council for their lifetimes and were not replaced when they died. Hiawatha was supposedly rewarded with

1. Iroquoian chief's headdress with deer antlers, late 19th century. The honours of the deer were the symbol of prestigious office. [WICEC] 2. Mrs. George Green, Turtle Clan Mother for the Upper Cayuga longhouse, ca. 1950. [WICEC]

1.

2.

this office as well as Joseph Brant and Red Jacket, two famous pine tree chiefs at the end of the 18th and the beginning of the 19th centuries.

The Confederacy was a complex system of government with a built-in system of checks and balances. It was not the intention of a structure to rule and/or control the people; rather its purpose was to represent them and secure their participation. All chiefs were equal in rank and authority. Their powers were held jointly with the Confederacy. Control of the confederacy council by any one or combination of nations was kept in check by the main principle of the one common thread of the nations — their religion. The primary principle of reciprocity, supported by their religion, influenced all aspects of their form of government including the seating arrangement in council which was divided into two sides or moieties. Unanimity was a fundamental law of the league and source of its strength.

The league itself was viewed as a major institution within the community as is evident by a number of symbolic references used over the years to describe its significance. It was sometimes referred to as an imaginary longhouse with each part occupied by one of the Five Nations. Since the original Iroquois territory lay in an east-west direction from the Great Lakes to the Hudson Valley, each tribe lived in adjacent sections. The Mohawks became the "Keepers of the Eastern Door", the Senecas the "Keepers of the Western Door", and the Onondagas "Keepers of Council Fire." The metaphor served to reinforce the feeling of unity inherent in the idea of living together in a communal longhouse. Various beaded wampum belts, also symbolic, celebrated the league in beaded geometric designs, the most popular symbol being the majestic image of the Great White Pine tree with its four white roots extending to the four directions. The tree of the long leaves signified the law or constitution of the union. The branches signified the shelter, protection and security that was to be found in the union. The white roots which stretched to the four directions symbolized the extension of the law and peace to all nations who wished to be members of it. The eagle, perched on top of the white pine, became a symbol of the watchfulness that the people must have to warn the people should the Confederacy be threatened.

It is understandable that the principles, practice and philosophy of the Confederacy were examined by other political powers. In fact, the constitution of the United States of America, the Marxist theory of Communism and formation of the League of Nations (United Nations) all have referred to the structural basis of the original Confederacy established centuries ago by Deganawidah.

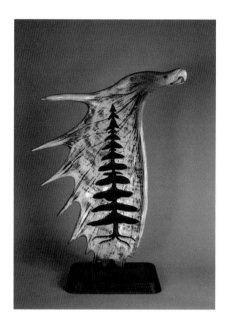

Tree of Peace (1981). The Great White Pine, its branches signifying shelter, its roots extending to the four directions symbolizing the desire for peace to all nations, is a major symbol in Iroquoian mythology. [WICEC]

Two worlds collide

The history of the colonization of the St. Lawrence lowlands by the Europeans, particularly the French, then the British, is an important part of Indian history, but it is rarely seen from the Indian point of view. The Algonkians enabled the early French explorers to survive and succeed in the New World. They provided food and shelter, methods of transportation such as the toboggans, snowshoes and the birchbark canoe. They taught the early immigrants how to grow food, how to hunt and fish and how to cure their

Algonkian Birchbark Canoe. The early fur traders were indebted to Canada's native peoples who supplied the sleek birch bark canoe for quick mobility over the waterway highways spread out like a huge fish net across the Canadian Shield. [*WICEC*]

sick. The Algonkian and Iroquoian Nations neither feared nor felt inferior to the arriving Europeans.

The New World and its inhabitants revolutionized the European world view by becoming a symbol of hope for a Europe emerging from centuries of overcrowding, poverty and religious persecution. Here was a nation — or as the early explorers found out — a variety of nations which did not fit the European conception of what a nation should be. The new peoples they encountered shared none of their cultural background. Indians had their own ideas about property ownership, leadership and warfare. Their own particular world view came into direct confrontation with Europeans unable to share such concepts. They thus set about to change the Indians through Christianity.

In 1534, Jacques Cartier became the first of many explorers to sail the St. Lawrence. There he found an untapped source of furs among Indians who were willing to trade for European goods. As the fur trade developed and matured, it had a profound impact on the Iroquoian and Algonkian nations living in the St. Lawrence lowlands. With the fur trade came the Jesuit missionaries, epidemics, military outposts, settlers and the competition for land and furs.

Competition between the British and French led to the competition among Indian Nations. It became the primary factor for the many wars that raged along the St. Lawrence. The Algonkian-speaking Montagnais, Naskaspi, Abnakis, Micmacs, Crees and Ojibways as well as the Iroquoian-speaking Hurons and Neutrals all became involved in complex fur trading relationships with the French. These trading relationships remained until the mid-17th century when the Iroquois Confederacy became truly unified and aligned itself with the British against the French.

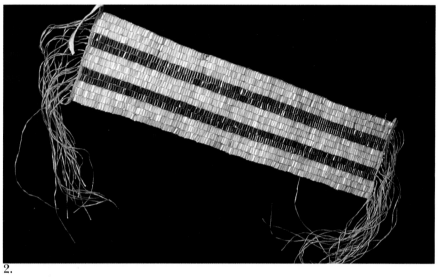

2.

1.
1. *This Silver Communion Service was sent by Queen Anne for use in the Mohawk Chapel.at Fort Hunter in upper New York.Following their meeting, in 1710, in England, four Mohawk "kings" requested Anglican missionaries for their people.* [*WICEC*] 2. *Gus-wen-tah. This Two row Wampum Belt records, in coded form, a formal agreement between the Indian and European nations, first made with the Dutch in the early 16th century.* [*WICEC*]

The Confederacy brought with them to the British the Gus-wen-tah or the Two-Row Wampum Belt which in codified form recorded a formal agreement between the two nations. The Gus-wen-tah was first made with the Dutch in the middle of the 16th Century.

The belt consists of two rows of purple wampum beads on a white background or bed. Three rows of white beads symbolizing peace, friendship and respect separate the two purple rows. The two purple rows symbolized two paths or two vessels travelling down the same river. One row symbolized Indian people with their law, their customs and their ways; the other row symbolized Europeans laws, customs and ways. Both paths or vessels move side by side in the same direction and neither interferes with one another. The principles of the two-row wampum became the basis for all treaties and agreements that were made with the Europeans.

The Iroquois Confederacy held the balance of power and maintained a supreme position both geographically and politically. The Queen Ann Silver Communion Service and Bible, given to four Mohawk Chiefs and one Mohican in 1710 in England, was just one of many symbolic gifts to the Confederacy to ensure their alliance to the British.

Once the British gained control of North America from the French, the position of power of the Iroquois Confederacy began to wane. No longer could the League play one Nation against another.

By the time the American Revolutionary War broke out, the Confederacy was so disoriented that the laws of unanimity within the council no longer prevailed. The Tuscaroras (who joined the league in 1712) and the Oneidas sided with the Americans while the Cayugas, Senecas, Onondagas and Mohawks under the leadership of Joseph Brant supported the British. Although the Onondagas remained by tradition the senior tribe in council, it was the Mohawk

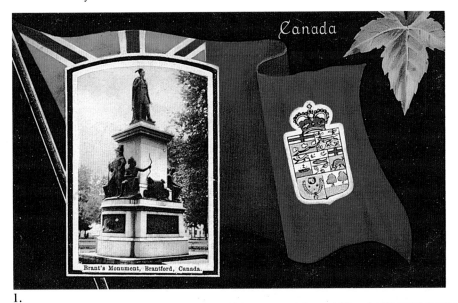

1.

1. *Monument to Chief Joseph Brant at Brantford, unveiled in 1886 by the Hon. J.B. Robinson, Lieutenant Governor of Ontario. [C.J. Humber]* 2. *Queen Elizabeth II signing the historic Queen Anne Bible in St. Paul's Chapel of the Mohawks, Brantford, during the Ontario Bicentennial, 1984. Chief Wellington Staats and Mrs. Staats are with Her Majesty. [WICEC]*

2.

Nation which dominated the external relationships with the British government.

After the American Revolution, the pro-British Six Nations followed Joseph Brant to the Grand River in Canada. General Frederick Haldimand, then Governor-in-Chief of Canada and the Crown's representative, issued a proclamation on October 25, 1784, granting a tract of land, estimated at 675,000 acres, which lay six miles deep on each side of the Grand River from its mouth to its source. Each nation established its own village and council house along the river, but it was the Mohawk Village, the home of Joseph Brant, that gained prominence. By 1791, Mohawk Village had a chapel, a school, a grist mill, a councilhouse and well-constructed houses for approximately 250 residents. Once the village was established, life in the village acquired a comfortable style of living relative to other Loyalist settlements not far from the village; the Mohawks were exceptionally well-off.

After the War of 1812, the Mohawk Village began to decline as many of its male residents died in the war. Joseph Brant moved out of the village in 1802 and died in 1807. After his death the British government's interest in the village waned. By 1861, Mohawk

1. *Sir Frederick Haldimand (1718-1791), Canada's Governor-in-Chief, granted land to the loyal Six Nations Indians along the Grand River. Painting by Lemuel F. Abbott. [Royal Ontario Museum, Canadiana Gallery] 2. Tyendinaga Council House, Mohawk Reserve, near Deseronto, ca. 1900. [C.J. Humber] 3. Mohawk Village, 1794, from a drawing by Elizabeth Simcoe. [Ontario Archives] 4. Mohawk Indian Church (1785), Brantford, Ontario, one of the oldest wooden structures in Canada. Chief Joseph Brant's tomb is inset in upper left. [C.J. Humber]*

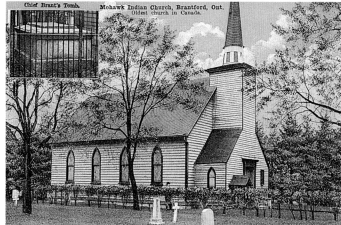

2.

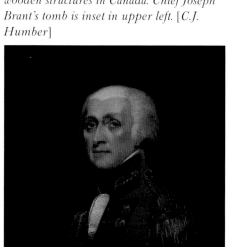

3.

4.

Village was inhabited by only one household and the lands surrounding the village came under the administrative office of the Church of England.

Slowly the Iroquoian Confederacy re-emerged as the governing body on the reserve which now occupied only about 45,000 acres of the original 675,000 land grant. From 1840, through to the end of World War I, the reserve community grew and prospered. Traditional Iroquoian social, religious, and political institutions continued; however, new organizations were developed to meet the needs of the changing times. For example, several Six Nations farmers formed the Six Nations Agricultural Society in 1867 and by 1883 held their annual fall fair in the newly constructed exhibition hall in Ohsweken. In the field of education, the Six Nations School Board was established in 1877 with representatives from the Confederacy Council, local Anglican clergy and the local Indian agent managing eight reserve schools.

1. *Six Nations Confederacy Council, ca. 1890, showing Chief David John holding wampum belt.* [*WICEC*] 2. *Christ Church Tyendinaga, ca. 1890. This chapel is the custodian of one half of the communion silver set given to the Mohawks by Queen Anne in 1710.* [*C.J. Humber*]. 3. *Six Nations School SS 8. One of the reserve schools, near Brantford, Ontario, operated by the Six Nations School Board founded by the Confederacy of Six Nations.* [*WICEC*] 4. *Six Nations Council House, Ohsweken, near Brantford, Ontario, ca. 1910.* [*C.J. Humber*]

1.

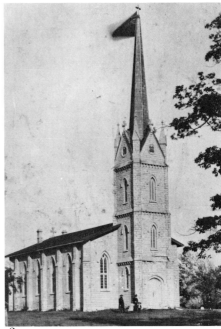

2.

3.

4.

Through successive generations, the Iroquois people at Six Nations fulfilled their loyalist obligations, participating in war after war as allies of the British Crown. After the Great War, the Canadian Government instituted a municipal style of government, replacing the Confederacy which still exists today but has very limited political scope.

In the years just before Canada's own Confederation, Great Britain began transferring control of Indian matters to Canada. By 1868 the first Indian Act was passed formalizing control over all Indian matters including the establishment of Indian lands as reserves. Today, there are seven Algonkian and seven Iroquoian reserve communities in the St. Lawrence lowlands.

It is difficult to represent adequately all the cultural and historical information of all of the 14 Iroquoian and Algonkian reserves, since there are so many differences in the historical development, culture, resources and geographic location of their communities. All of the communities reluctantly accepted the consequences of the dominant society and made efforts to adopt their own rules of conduct and their own philosophy into their new lifestyles. Although much has been lost, there still remains alive today a vital Indian culture. In the realm of fine arts, Indian esthetics has influenced the whole development of the modern art movement and revitalized the culture with a new Indian identity. Traditional religion, which was never lost on a few Iroquoian reserves, has become more relevant to technological societies with its philosophy of coexistence with the natural environment.

There is no typical reserve. Generally speaking, the Indian reserves situated in Southern Ontario and Quebec are all near major commercial and industrial centres with good opportunities for employment. Many of the men from Tyendinaga, St. Regis, New

1. Brigadier O.M. Martin of the Six Nations Reserve is representative of the many hundreds of Woodland Indians of the St. Lawrence Valley who fought for King and Country during the Great Wars of this century. [WICEC] 2. Battalion banner from the First Great War showing clan symbols of Six Nations. Special permission was granted by His Majesty George V for its use. [WICEC] 3. Cadets on parade at the Mohawk Institute, today the headquarters for the Woodland Indian Cultural Educational Centre in Brantford. [WICEC]

1.

2.

3.

Credit, Caughnawaga and Six Nations are eagerly sought after in high steel construction. The Mohawks of Caughnawaga have been especially recognized for their work on the UN Building, R.C.A. Building and the Empire State Building in New York. Some reserves such as Tyendinaga have over the years developed excellent farming communities.

Educated and well-trained individuals have made notable achievements in the arts, politics, sports, civil service, academia, law, and science. E. Pauline Johnson, the celebrated Mohawk poetess; Alanis Obonsawin, a noted filmmaker from Odanak; Max Gros-Louis, Huron Chief and founder of the Indian Association of Quebec; Dr. Oronhyatekha, a Mohawk from Deseronto, who as Supreme Chief put the Independent Order of Foresters on the world map; Alwyn Morris, Mohawk kayaker from Caughnawaga and winner of a Gold Medal at the Los Angeles Olympics; Rick Beaver, a well-known wild life artist and illustrator from Alderville; Dr. Gilbert Montour, a noted mining engineer and consultant to the United Nations; and Stan Jonathan, a celebrated former NHL player with the Boston Bruins are just a few representatives of the Indians of the St. Lawrence lowlands who have excelled in their chosen fields.

During the 1980's, a series of meetings were convened involving Canada's Prime Minister, provincial premiers and Indian First Nations, including representatives from the St. Lawrence Lowlands. Efforts were made by all participants to clarify Indian rights, particularly the right to self-government. Although these efforts did not meet with complete success, they began a process of negotiations which must ultimately be concluded.

We will then have come full circle and once again our culture will flourish as it was meant to be in the legacy of our ancestors...

1. *Mohawk high-steel climbers, almost totally lacking in fear of heights, are widely employed in structural steel work. Here they are seen atop the 222 foot tower of the Empire State Building which was added in 1951. Mohawks also helped to erect the 1,250 foot building in the early 1930s. [National Geographic Society]* 2. *Close-up of above.* 3. *Mohawks making lacrosse sticks, St. Regis Reserve, near Cornwall, Ontario, ca. 1900. [C.J. Humber]* 4. *Alanis Obonsawin, singer, arts administrator and film maker from the Odanak Indian Reserve in Quebec. [WICEC]* 5. *Oronhyatekha (1841-1907), or Peter Martin, one of the most outstanding Iroquoians since Chief Joseph Brant. A physician, and graduate of Oxford University, he made fraternal benevolence his lifework. As Supreme Chief Ranger of the IOOF, elected in 1881, he greatly increased its membership and international influence. [Independent Order of Foresters]*

4.

5.

The Woodland Indians
Elizabeth McLuhan

Paul Kane painter/peintre **Canada 7**

Stamp: *"Indian Encampment on Lake Huron". This Paul Kane (1810-1871) painting depicts a typical Woodland Indian setting, ca. 1850.* [*Canada Post Corporation*]

Native peoples known as Woodland Indians trace their beginnings back 3000 years. Their culture grew out of an earlier period known as the archaic phase which extends back even further from three to seven thousand years ago. It was in the archaic period that the woodland lifestyle of hunting, fishing and gathering emerged.

Both Cree and Ojibway Indians inhabited the woodland area of Manitoba, central and northern Ontario, and Quebec. The Cree and Ojibway are members of the larger Algonkian linguistic family. In Canada, they inhabit an Eastern woodland environment north and west of the Great Lakes extending from Manitoba to Quebec. Both Cree and Ojibway hunted, fished and gathered food in the richly forested and plentifully endowed lake region. The men hunted alone or in small groups while the women gathered the food.

They lived in small family groups during the winter months and gathered together in villages during the summer months. Their residences often were dome-shaped dwellings covered with sheets of birchbark. For transportation, they used birchbark or dugout canoes, snowshoes, tumplines, and toboggans. Tools included bone knives, a form of crooked knife, stone scrapers, wooden fire drills, and mallet and pitch spreaders for canoe-making.

The socio-political organization was loose. The largest unit was the band, linked by language, kinship and clanship. The most basic unit, however, was the extended family hunting group, each of which had its own recognized hunting territory. Although each band designated a chief, his power was relatively limited.

Contact with Europeans occurred as early as the 16th century. Directly or indirectly, the Cree and Ojibway traded fur in exchange for rifles, steel knives and manufactured goods. As this trade developed, inter-tribal warfare became more intense. The Ojibway moved southward displacing their long-standing enemy, the Sioux, and eastward where they came into conflict with the Iroquois. Bands tended to settle and hunt near trading routes and centres. From 1760 to 1820, a common Indian-European material culture emerged. This culture was heavily dependent upon European supplies.

After 1820, game began to grow scarce. The new English settlers were more interested in land than furs. The Cree and Ojibway, once important middle men, were left dependent upon European goods and now lacked a trade item. Gradually, the bands passed under treaties and were relegated to reserves. The intensity of European influence and the progress of assimilation varied from reserve to

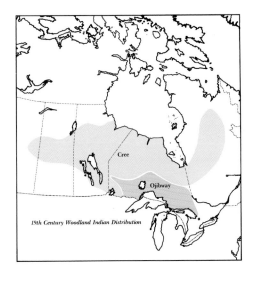

19th Century Woodland Indian Distribution

Cree

Ojibway

1.

1. *"Interior of a Cree Indian Tent."* Hand-coloured Engraving by Robert Hood (1796-1821). [*Public Archives of Canada* [*PAC*]/*D-38951*] 2. *Woodland "Indian Encampment." Water Colour and Gouache by William Armstrong (1822-1914). Probably St. Marys River at present day site of Sault Ste. Marie.* [*PAC/C-40328*] 3. *"Fort William, 1865" showing Woodland Indian Encampment. Water Colour, by William Armstrong.* [*PAC/C-10512*]

2.

3.

reserve. Each reserve developed slightly different adaptations to the new environment of European culture. Initially, much of the social and economic life of the native community focussed upon the trading post. By mid-19th century, the mission with its school and a new corps of government administrators, teachers and doctors, became central to the community. Hunting and trapping had become less and less profitable and old ways were lost. Employment on the reserves was scarce and gradually the welfare system, as it exists today, took a firm grip on Indian life.

Crafts played an important role in Cree and Ojibway life. Both Cree and Ojibway finger-painted and used the loom to create a variety of woven items such as bands, sashes, garters and straps. Geometric designs used in weaving ranged from stripes and triangles to zigzags and saw-tooth. By the 20th century, traditional weaving techniques had largely disappeared. Currently, however, there is a revival of interest in weaving in Ontario native communities.

White birchbark was a vital construction material in Cree and Ojibway crafts. With its varying thickness, it could be torn off easily and straight. It was durable and provided protection against weather. The strongest bark, called winter bark, was collected in spring. Summer bark was thinner and easier to remove. The thinnest bark was used as wrapping.

The largest pieces of sturdy bark were set aside for the construction of large canoes. Smaller pieces of bark were shaped into containers of varying shapes, which could be made water-tight. To make these *makuks*, a single piece of bark was bent while it was being steamed over a hot fire. Seams were sewn with roots or fibres. Gum or pitch was used to seal openings.

Makuks were often decorated with scratched or peeled designs. These design figures were outlined on the container and the background peeled off to reveal a lighter inner bark. This process could

1. *Cree Hunter Calling Moose, from Curtis, E.S., The North American Indian… (1926). [PAC/C-20844]* 2. *Woodland Indian family, Montreal River, North of Sault Ste. Marie. The transition from tipi to contemporary home is evident in this crudely constructed log dwelling, ca. 1905. [Charles J. Humber Collection]* 3. *Ojibway Indians at Osnaburgh House, Ontario, 1929. [PAC/PA-20303]*

1.

2.

3.

be reversed, subtracting the main design figure and leaving the background a darker contrasting bark.

Few decorated *makuks* have been made in Ontario since the turn of the 20th century. Quilled decorated bark containers are still being produced in a few locations in Ontario, most notably on Parry Island and Manitoulin Island. These boxes display rich adornment and dyed quills painstakingly applied to the lid and sides.

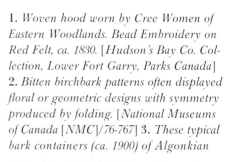

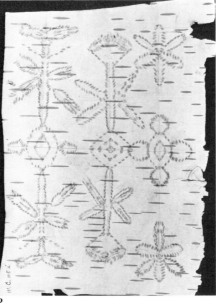

1. 2. 4.

5. 6.

Birchbark designs and quillwork, both traditional and contemporary, may be said to demonstrate a propensity for dramatically contrasting figure and ground. This contrast was achieved through the use of positive/negative space of peeled design, sharply varying textures of quill and bark, and bright primary colours.

Designs were both freehand and traced, as in beadwork. Often ideas were taken from birchbark bitten patterns or transparencies. Depending upon how many times a piece of bark was folded over, a symmetrical design of two, four, or more units would be produced.

1. *Woven hood worn by Cree Women of Eastern Woodlands. Bead Embroidery on Red Felt, ca. 1830.* [*Hudson's Bay Co. Collection, Lower Fort Garry, Parks Canada*] 2. *Bitten birchbark patterns often displayed floral or geometric designs with symmetry produced by folding.* [*National Museums of Canada* [*NMC*]/*76-767*] 3. *These typical bark containers (ca. 1900) of Algonkian origin illustrate the peeled-design technique.* [*Woodland Indian Cultural Educational Centre* [*WICEC*]] 4. *Comtemporary Ojibway Quill Boxes, Parry Sound, Ontario.* [*Dept. of Indian and Northern Affairs* [*DINA*]] 5. *Traditional Woodland Indian Birchbark Canoe, Under Construction at Fort William, Thunder Bay, Ontario.* [*Ontario Ministry of Citizenship and Culture*] 6. *Birchbark container, makuk, made from birch bent by steaming and sewn with roots or fibres, ca. 1840.* [*C.J. Humber; Photo/ David de Verteuil*]

These thin transparent pieces were used as a means of design experimentation or as models for actual work in another medium. Bitten patterns frequently displayed geometric and floral designs simultaneously. Moose hair embroidery bore great resemblance to quillwork and was often used in conjunction with it, or alone. Techniques and style of embroidery on birchbark or clothing were much the same as those of quill design. Today the skill has disappeared.

Clothing was very important and much time was devoted to its ornamentation. Clothes, well-decorated, became a matter of prestige. Hides of deer, moose, caribou, bear and elk were carefully tanned and tailored into pouches, moccasins, leggings, breech-clouts, and vests. All techniques were employed: embroidery, quillwork, beadwork, ribbon applique.

1.

2.

3.

1. Ojibway Vest. Black velveteen accentuates the colourful design. Beaded clothing signified status and prestige. [Royal Ontario Museum, Toronto] 2. Contemporary Moose Hair Embroidery on Hide, with Fur Trim. [National Museums of Canada/J-21608] 3. This contemporary example of Ojibway beadwork demonstrates design intricacy. [DINA]

Soon after contact with European culture, broadcloth became available and quickly supplanted hides. Colours of red, deep blues and black were preferred by the Cree and Ojibway as backgrounds for a colourful array of applied design. In the 19th century, the Ojibway adopted dark velveteen, usually black, despite its higher price. Black velveteen dramatically accentuated the now predominantly beaded patterns of leggings, vests, sleeves and bandoliers, and moccasins. By the late 19th century, Ojibway design reached a rococo frenzy of undulating lines and bright and contrasting colours.

In a sense, decorative beadwork experienced a sort of inflation. Just as Northwest Coast totem poles grew in size and elaboration with the availability of new tools, and the influx of increased numbers of goods into the economy, so beaded clothing came to signify status and prestige — the more beadwork, the greater the prestige.

Beads were woven in bands on looms or applied in a couched stitch directly to the material. The work of the 18th and early 19th century displayed geometric designs and conventionalized flowers and leaves. These "semi-realistic" forms were flexible in their arrangement and subdued in their colours. However, by the mid-19th century, the floral design predominated and flowers and leaves grew larger and brighter.

Ojibway beadwork of the 19th century became more linear, more prone to multiple outlines of contrasting colour and elaborate veining of stems or petals. The most outstanding feature of new design developments was the increased movement within these floral patterns. Cree beadwork also flourished during the 19th century and underwent similar transformations.

The 20th century in Ontario saw a decline in the decorative arts. Currently a revival of a number of craft skills, including beadwork and quillwork, is underway. These, however, are not for domestic use but for sale as tourist and craft items, to a non-native public.

The religion of the Cree-Ojibway today may be described as an amalgam of Christianity and native beliefs. Traditionally, the Cree-Ojibway shared much in common with the religion of other woodland groups, although rituals and social structures may have differed. Above all, traditional religion recognized one Great Spirit or Manitou who was neither good nor bad. He had no real name or associated form in which he appeared. He was assumed to be above the earth and hence was sometimes identified with the sky, symbolized by the sun, source of life and nourishment. Without the Great Spirit, all would perish and life forces would cease to flow.

In the creation myth, man came last. He was totally dependent upon those animals and plants which had preceded him. In order to survive, man had to flow within the natural cycle and to co-operate with the various spirits. There was a fine and reverent attitude towards life's delicate balance and a sensitivity to the spirits within it.

Spirits were invisible, but could manifest themselves in any number of forms. Man, according to early belief, lived simultaneously on a number of levels corresponding to the levels of being

1.

2.

1. *Contemporary Ojibway Beadwork Loom. Beads were woven on looms or applied in a couch stitch directly to the material.* [*DINA*] 2. *The old tradition of making band boxes still lives in the Ojibway region of Parry Sound, Ontario.* [*DINA*]

within each man. Man's body appears and perishes, but his "soul" travels to another land. The soul included the idea of the heart or spirit of a man. It was located in the chest, roughly where the heart is. There was also the more ephemeral shadow which bridged the bodily and non-bodily. This shadow was thought to stay near the grave after physical death.

Cree-Ojibway religion was greatly concerned with the acquisition of power. Traditionally, the spirit quest extended into the woodland and subarctic areas. Guided by an older, wiser man, an Indian youth would undergo isolation and strict fasting to induce a state conducive to the visitation of a spirit or vision. This vision would provide him with the key to his actions and a guardian spirit which he had to follow. In turn, the guardian spirit would help him when he called upon it.

Dreams were considered omens, and sources of further power. Accumulated power could be used against others in the form of witchcraft. The Cree and Ojibway perceived that illness, death and accidents had natural causes, but they also held that these misfortunes could be caused by the evil machinations of someone else directing the forces of nature. Powerful individuals such as these frequently became shamans. Shamans performed rituals to secure spiritual assistance or cures for the ailing. Both Cree and Ojibway performed the Shaking Tent ceremony. This ceremony took place in a small conical hut which, because of the power concentrated within by the shaman, would rise and shake violently.

Individuals seeking further power could also apply for membership to the Midewiwin or Grand Medicine Society. The Midewiwin Society was a highly sophisticated medico-religious society that preserved and passed along a vast store of plant and herbal lore for the purpose of securing good health and curing illness. This society also demanded a high moral code, and taught the correct path of life. Individuals could pass through eight grades or degrees, the first four, Earth Midewiwin, and the next four, Sky Midewiwin. The last four were considered the most powerful. Birchbark scrolls recorded both the various stages through which the initiate passed and the transfer of power which had occurred.

With the introduction of Christianity, the native spirits did not disappear, nor were they denied an existence. Christian beliefs, then, were superimposed upon already existing native beliefs. Over the years, the two have been compartmentalized to serve various functions.

Cree and Ojibway created pictographic records for both sacred and secular functions. Religious pictographs were used for the private dream images of spirit questers and for the Midewiwin

Midewiwin Birchbark Scroll, Kenora, Ontario. Midewiwin Society members employed a loose system of pictographic etching on birchbark scrolls to act as aide-mémoire. [NMC]

Society. Secular pictographs, meant to convey information to all, took the form of maps, messages to travellers, totemic identification as on grave-boards, and casual story-telling.

The young spirit quester, having achieved a vision, would make some sort of representation, carved or painted, and keep it with him, first upon his body, later in his Midewiwin medicine bag. Bark records of the Midewiwin Society were mnemonic devices which helped preserve the traditions of society. As a pictorial résumé of the history of the Midewiwin, these records were kept hidden from common view and were unrolled only when a candidate was ready to be advanced. The scrolls themselves were large strips of heavy birchbark, often pieced together to reach up to eight feet in length.

By the nature of its materials and tools, scroll work was sketchy and fine-lined. Frequently the figures were delicate and detailed to a surprising degree. The overall effect of the bark scrolls is one of extreme lightness, of a finely wrought openwork.

Sacred power or a figure from the supernatural realm was indicated by a series of lines emanating from the depicted figure. These interconnecting lines or determinatives could be straight or wavy. The meaning of these determinatives could be broadened to include those lines which extended from one figure to another, to indicate power relationships or sensory perception between them. This network of lines greatly enlarged the range of expression, more precisely defined interrelationships, and allowed for greater complexity in the abstract content of the scrolls.

The Midewiwin scroll outlined an architectural groundplan, a procedural blueprint based on the lodge's symbolic construction and layout. Arrangement of the figures was determined by the degree to which the candidate was to be advanced. Coloured posts placed at intervals marked the progressive degrees of the ceremony from one end of the lodge to the other. This architectural/procedural model was also a cosmological model of the Cree-Ojibway religion. The model represented the archetypal spiritual journey or path of the initiate and included the possible pitfalls and the forces of good and evil that the initiate would have to face.

Vertical waving lines moving upwards, from a body, or part of a body, short bristly lines, or clusters of dots, all implied spiritual power. Horned figures, animal or human, suggested power. In the case of humans, these lines indicated power to the degree of a shaman.

Transfer of energy or power was an important subject of the Midewiwin scrolls. The network of lines conveyed both a perpetual movement of power, and a stabilization of formal design. The linear determinatives simultaneously confirmed the separateness

Midewiwin Birchbark Scroll. The scroll was both a ceremonial blueprint and cosmological overview. Each scroll could be interpreted accurately only by its author and initiate. Because of the sacred nature of the scrolls, museums that may possess examples do not exhibit them. [Royal Ontario Museum [ROM]]

of figures and united them in a shared rhythmical response pattern. The pattern was further unified by the overall architectural framework.

Pictography used for secular purposes was not concerned with the transfer of power. Although secular pictography bore a general resemblance to religious pictography, the system of sacred notations or determinatives was absent in secular pictographs.

Rock paintings may be seen in abundance in the Great Lakes and Canadian Shield region and are the most distinctive legacy of the Woodland Indians. Though of undetermined origin, these paintings bear a remarkable similarity in vocabulary of form to that of the Cree-Ojibway scroll pictography.

Executed in a red pigment that cannot be reproduced today, these paintings were created on vertical rock faces close to the water. The pigment was probably applied by hand or fingers. This red ochre has endured to this day on the cliff walls. The binding agent is still not known. The figures portrayed in rock paintings ranged from identifiable game animals to human beings to more ambiguous geometric symbols.

The exact age of these paintings cannot be determined. It is estimated, however, that some are over 1000 years old, judging from the plant overgrowth. These paintings were accessible to an artist standing or sitting in his canoe. In some instances, there was a ledge upon which to balance.

The style of these paintings, like that of the scrolls, was abstract. The depiction of animals was frequently naturalistic. Human figures tended to be stylized, geometric abbreviations. Determinatives were found also on the rock figures in the form of horns or bristles. The cast of characters was similar to that of the scrolls.

Algonkian rock characters rarely overlapped. Often natural rock formations were incorporated into the design. These paintings are thought to have been made by spirit questers and medicine men. They were considered sacred in themselves, for even today small offerings may be found on nearby ledges.

From the decorative arts to pictography, the art of the Woodland Indians shares certain formal characteristics. One such characteristic is the use of contrasting textures and bright primary colours to enhance both figure and ground. Another is the use of outlines to help define a given character.

The vocabulary or form of the pictographic records may have been a source from which decorative designs were sometimes derived. However, the important distinction between the two was that the real subject of pictography — *the transfer of power* — was forbidden to the crafts. Determinatives, largely a tool to portray power

1.

2.

1. *Pictograph — Mishipizhiw, Also Known as an Underwater Serpent in the Cree/ Ojibway Tradition. Upper Great Lakes.*

2. *"Mounted Horseman", Pictograph, Agawa Site, Northern Ontario. The most distinctive legacy of the Woodland Indians are the various rock paintings found in the Great Lakes and Canadian Shield regions.*

relationships, were confined to scrolls or rock art. Ceremonial objects were also allowed to bear religious iconography.

The decorative arts, with the exception of weapons, were largely the domain of women. Although traditionally women could create ceremonial designs on appropriate objects, a man's weapon could not be touched by any woman.

Craft designs were not considered sacred in themselves. Certain secular designs became associated with particular individuals or families through repetition and time. These designs may be described as having been in a popular idiom and were familiar to the craftswoman's community. Today, certain craft traditions are being continued in Ontario. Finished products are no longer for domestic use, but for tourist and craft sale at distant outlets.

Midewiwin scrolls were created by and for society members. Although scroll pictography was elaborate, it was not standardized. Each scroll could be interpreted accurately only by its author and initiate. The scroll served as an architectural and procedural blueprint and became the sacred property of the new member. Because of the sacred nature of the scrolls, museums that may possess examples do not exhibit them.

Images, other than decorative forms, were of a spiritual nature, such as those of the young spirit questers. They were expressions of the conveyance of power. This power could be directed for good or ill. Even out of context, these images were thought to retain power. They were not for commercial sale or public view. Unlike decorative patterns, the religious images were created by people who possessed and controlled spiritual power.

For this reason, the initial reaction by native people to Norval Morrisseau's work was suspicious and sometimes violent. His use of the power symbols suggested his control of power, his ability to use it for witchcraft purposes. His paintings made public that which was considered sacred and privileged information.

Like contemporary crafts, these images are no longer created for the artists' own use. The role of artist is viewed as an end in itself, as a full-time job, as a means of achieving dignity in the white world. This new art does, however, serve the native community by attempting to change non-native attitudes towards native people.

The model that Morrisseau provided is a vital bridge between two cultures and dramatically updates traditional pictographic and design forms for the contemporary art market. By bridging these cultures, Morrisseau, the artist, and the many Indian painters who followed him have contributed to the spirit of cultural revitalization evident in many Indian communities today.

Norval Morrisseau: Artist at Work. Morris-seau, born of Ojibway ancestry in 1932, is the originator of the pictographic style or what is sometimes referred to as the Woodland Indian style, a fusion of Midewiwin Society scrolls and native Indian rock painting. He is the first Indian to break through the Canadian professional art barrier and is truly a giant in the Canadian art world. [DINA]

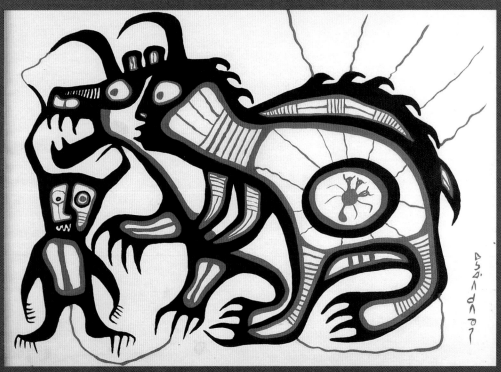

1.

1. "Untitled, 1967" Morrisseau.
A human figure within an animal frequently indicated the spiritual authority of the animal, not the literal swallowing of one by another. [DINA/151784] 2. "Thunderbird and Snake", Norval Morrisseau, n.d. The themes of transformation and of the conflict between good and evil recur throughout Morrisseau's 25 year career. The artist's Indian name means "Copper Thunderbird" and the thunderbird has served as a spiritual and visual talisman for the artist. [DINA/84-0506]

2.

1.

CANADA's Native Peoples

1. *"Rhythm of the Drum", Daphne Odjig, 1977. The visual depiction of movement and sound has become Odjig's hallmark. Her stylistic freedom makes her form unmistakable and innovative.* [DINA/85-0042]
2. *Born on the Wikwemikong Reserve on Manitoulin Island, Odjig's work since the mid-60s has focused on several ceremonies at the heart of Ojibway spiritualism.* [DINA] *Native art in Canada is flourishing as Canada's Woodland Indians express in art form the legacy of their forbears:* 3. *Bob Bellegarde;* 4. *Jackson Beardy;* 5. *Alex Janvier;* 6. *Arthur Shilling.* [3-6, DINA]

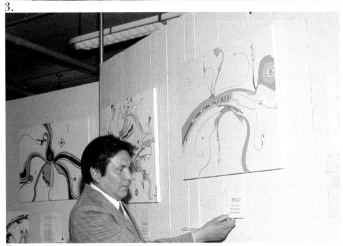

2.

3.

4.

5.

6.

The Plains Indian Nations of Western Canada
Ian Getty

The Indian nations of the western Canadian Plains have been a vital part of the prairie landscape for thousands of years. In the 19th century the "plains culture area" encompassed: the vast buffalo range lands of the parkland-foothills of the Rocky Mountains, where the Mountain Stoneys roamed; the Sarcee, Blackfoot, Blood and Peigan territory in central and southern Alberta; the prairie flat lands of Saskatchewan, shared by the Plains Cree and Assiniboine tribes; and western Manitoba where more Cree and some Sioux bands shared the buffalo plains with the Plains Ojibway (Saulteaux) bands.

A rich and colourful diversity exists among the different Prairie peoples who are grouped linguistically into three major language groups: Algonkian, Athapaskan and Siouan. The Algonkian speakers — the Blackfoot, Cree, and Ojibway — comprise the largest population. The Siouan speakers are represented by the

Stamp: *The Plains Indians wore brightly coloured clothing for their ceremonial dances as portrayed on this Canada Post stamp from a painting by Blackfoot Indian Gerald Tailfeathers.*

Canada 8

Indians of Les Indiens
the Plains des Plaines

1.

1. *A Sarcee Indian family, ca. 1900.* [*Prov. Archives of Alberta. E. Brown Collection B 49*] **2.** *From "In the North-West with the Mounted Police," by Dr. R.B. Nevitt, 1881; this montage shows typical scenes among Blackfoot, Sarcee, Stoneys and Cree.* [*Glenbow Archives* [*GA*], *Calgary/5376*]

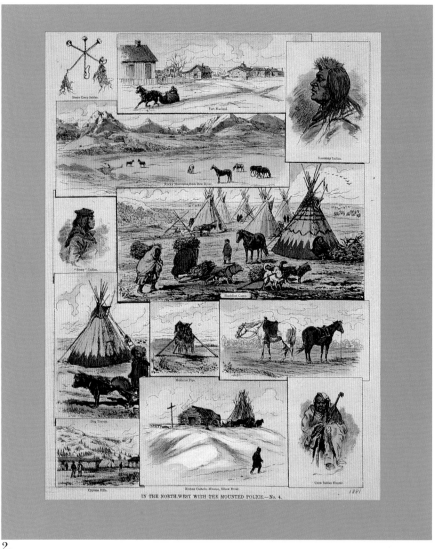

2.

Dakota Sioux of Manitoba and Saskatchewan, the Assiniboine of Saskatchewan, and the Stoneys of Alberta. The Sarcee Indians of southern Alberta, who reportedly split from the northern Beaver tribe, represent the Athapaskan linguistic family.

Plains Indian culture before European contact was based on hunting, fishing, gathering and inter-tribal trading. The harsh temperate climate restricted agriculture while the use of natural food plants depended on the specific area and the customs of the various tribes. The plains people travelled on foot and used dog travois until the early 18th century when the horse was re-introduced to the prairies. Indian technology included the bow and arrow, spears, snares and, most importantly, buffalo pounds and buffalo jumps. Buffalo, deer and elk were plentiful, and hence they were a source of clothing. Animal hide shelters (tipis) were easily constructed and portable. The social groupings generally consisted of small ex-

1. *A Blackfoot camp, ca. 1900, showing the use of travois as ladders to assist in the pinning together of the tipi hide cover.* [*C.J. Humber*] 2. *Plains Indian Shooting Buffalo, a main source of food for the Indians of the prairies for centuries.* [*Canada Post Corporation*] 3. *Cree, at the turn of the century, with travois, the main transportation device of Plains Indians.* [*C.J. Humber*] 4. *Mosawahoh, Loyal Sioux Indian from Prince Albert, ca. 1890.* [*John Young*]

1.

2.

3.

4.

39

tended families or bands of 50 to 100 members, guided by men recognized for their skills in hunting, oratory, religion or medicine. It was a difficult life closely attuned to the seasonal environment. Families and bands travelled great distances on hunting and trading expeditions.

The stereotypic eagle-fathered plains Indian warrior is often associated with the Sioux, originally a woodlands people inhabiting the forests of central Canada and north-eastern United States. When they migrated onto the plains they became skillful nomadic bison hunters. The Sioux tribes eventually dominated the headwaters of the Mississippi, Minnesota, and Missouri rivers. A northern group, before European contact, branched off, becoming identified as the Assiniboine, an Ojibwa term referring to their practice of boiling food by dropping heated rocks into water. Living along the length of the Assiniboine and Saskatchewan river systems, the Assiniboine remained strong allies of the Cree throughout the fur trade era. Together they became the middlemen in trading European goods to distant tribes. Later they became noted for their production of pemmican, the staple food for voyageurs and trading post employees. From an estimated population of 10,000 in the late 18th century, the Assiniboine were reduced to less than 3,000 within 100 years because of smallpox and other contagious diseases.

The Rocky Mountain Stoneys constitute another branch of the Sioux-Assiboine tribes. As they do today, they resided along the foothills from Chief Mountain in Montana to the Athabasca river in Jasper National Park. Anthropologists speculate that the Stoney bands — namely the Bearspaw, Chiniki and Wesley bands residing on the Morley reserve west of Calgary, and Paul's and Alexis bands west of Edmonton — possibly migrated west along the Saskatchewan river system as the fur trade expanded into the interior plains area. Stoney oral tradition recounts that some Stoney families have lived in the foothills since time immemorial; however, other elders tell of Stoney families fleeing the central plains of Montana to the

1. *The Stoney Indians of Alberta resided along the Rocky Mountain foothills. Here, at the base of Cascade Mountain, the moose tipi of John Hunter draws much attention from tourists attracted to the tipi village during the annual Banff Days early this century. [C.J. Humber]* 2. *A John Innes painting, ca. 1900, depicting Indians of the northern plains bringing furs to the local Hudson's Bay Trading Post.*

1.

2.

mountain foothills in order to escape the smallpox epidemics (recorded in the fur trade records as occurring around 1740, 1781 and 1830). Father de Smet, the Roman Catholic missionary travelling through the Bow Valley in 1840, reported that the Stoneys had separated from the Plains Assiniboine about 1790. These foothills-plains people hunted bison as well as other game animals. They traded furs, hides and fresh meat at the HBC posts at Rocky Mountain House and Edmonton House. They became invaluable guides to early explorers such as Capt. John Palliser and James Hector (1858-60), while assisting surveyors for the C.P.R. and Geological Survey of Canada. Converted to Methodism by Robert Rundle (1811-1896) in the 1840s, the Stoneys settled on their homelands near the Morleyville Methodist Mission established in 1873 by George and John McDougall along the Bow river. After signing Treaty No. 7 in 1877, the Stoney Nation continued to claim additional reserve lands and jealously preserved their traditional hunting and trapping rights. The Wesley court case of 1930 set a legal precedent for the recognition of hunting treaty rights in Canada. Eventually after years of fruitless petitions and frustrating negotiations, the government granted the Stoneys a 5,000 acre reserve at Bighorn (west of Nordegg) and the tribe purchased another 5,000 acre reserve at Eden Valley (west of Longview). Today the economic base of the people includes hunting, trapping, guiding, ranching, lumbering, handicraft sales and professional employment with their tribal government. As well, the Stoney bands operate commercial enterprises: gas stations, a Co-op store and restaurant, a health clinic, a conference lodge, and a campground. All these economic projects and services to band members have been financed from natural gas royalties which have amounted to millions in annual income.

1. *When hunting for buffalo and big game along the foothills, the Stoney family lived in the traditional tipi. [C.J. Humber]*
2. *"The Hand Game," 1961, by Gerald Tailfeathers (1925-1975). One of the first widely-recognized Native professional artists, Tailfeathers authentically portrayed life-scenes of his forbears, the Blackfoot; this game is a favourite past-time at pow-wows. [Glenbow Museum [GM], Calgary/7104]*
3. *Poundmaker Jr. and son [near Battleford, Sask.], 1896. They are descendants of Chief Poundmaker, a Cree leader jailed for his role in the 1885 Riel Rebellion. [G. Moodie, GA, Calgary]*

1.

2.

3.

1. *A significant 1908 pastel of "Wampekine-wap, Ojibway Indian" by Edmund Morris (1871-1913). This famous Ojibway warrior and medicine man was born in 1839 to Ojibway and Cree parents. He led his people against the Sioux, Blackfoot and Crow in tribal confrontations. [Royal Ontario Museum, Toronto]* 2. *With whip hanging from his arm, a treaty medal around his neck, a fringed bag with looking glass inside, and his hair tied in a ball, Crowfoot, the great Blackfoot Chief of the 19th century, sits for a ca. 1880 photo in Calgary. [John Young]* 3. *By A.J. Miller, "Rendez-vous" depicts the traditional annual gathering of Plains Indians in foothills of the Rocky Mountains during the last quarter of the 19th century. [Walters Art Gallery, Baltimore, Md.]*

2.

3.

1.

Like the Sioux, the Plains Cree were originally a woodland group who adopted the horse-bison culture. Their dialect and environment distinguished the Plains Cree from the Woodlands Cree (living in the Alberta and Saskatchewan parklands) and the Swampy Cree (living in the forests of Manitoba, northern Ontario and Quebec). Their social organization and religious belief were similar to other Plains Indian Nations. The Cree enjoyed the largest geographical distribution of any Indian Nation in western Canada and their efficiency as middlemen traders helped, in the 18th century, to ensure their position as the dominant tribe. Their economic well-being increasingly depended upon the annual fur harvest. By the 1800s, many Woods Cree took up residence near trading posts, adopting European goods, clothing and technology, while retaining their traditional social structures. Until the decline of the buffalo in the 1870s, the Plains Cree were more independent as they could rely on the bison herds.

The Cree controlled two vital resources necessary to the European trading companies — furs and to a lesser degree, fresh meat and pemmican. Their alliances with other tribes (notably Ojibway and Assiniboine) enabled them to expand rapidly into new territory, becoming the dominant group on the Saskatchewan plains. When the treaty commissioners arrived in the 1870s, the Cree were able to gain several significant concessions: increased annuity payments, promise of agricultural assistance, and the supply of a "medicine chest" for medical aid. Forced to live on reserves after the buffalo became extinct, they accepted farming and ranching while retaining their culture, language and identity. Opposing the Cree was the equally powerful Blackfoot Confederacy centred on the Red Deer, Bow and Old Man river systems of Alberta.

The most militant and feared of the Canadian plains Indians were the Blackfoot tribes comprised of the Blackfeet (Siksika), Blood (Kainai), and Peigan (Pekuni). Each tribe had its own chiefs and societies, but they united for some religious ceremonies, intermarried, and hunted or staged horse raids together. They did not become major participants in the fur trade economy until the early 19th century. In the north they supplied the HBC with buffalo dried pemmican, and in the south, they provided the American Fur Company with pemmican and buffalo robes. When the buffalo economy collapsed in the 1870s, the Blackfoot people became destitute within just three years of signing Treaty No. 7. The Siksika settled on their reserve at Blackfoot Crossing on the Bow river; the Bloods selected their reserve between the Belly and Old Man rivers in 1883 where over 3,000 members settled; the Peigan established their reserve near the Bloods on the Old Man River near Pincher Creek. A number of Blackfoot people became successful farmers and ranchers, but since World War II, the limited amount of reserve land and the rising population has forced hundreds to seek work and housing in nearby urban centres.

1. *The Horn Society of the Blood tribe was one of several important religious and military societies of the plains Blackfoot people. The secret rituals and ceremonies led to full rank of warrior. [C.J. Humber]*
2. *Medicine Lodges of Blackfoot (1907). The tipi was a portable home used year-round by Indians following buffalo herds. Sky and earth are represented by geometrical designs at top and bottom. Encircling the middle are symbols of personal guardian spirits as revealed in a vision to the owner. [C.J. Humber]*

1.

2.

The cross-cultural contacts resulting from the expansion of the fur trade onto the western plains significantly altered the Indians' way of life. The European traders — first the English, through the Hudson's Bay Company, and then the French-Canadian voyageurs, and later the North West Company (to 1821) became welcomed visitors to Indian territory. The Cree around James Bay initially dominated the fur trade in their role as "Homeguard Indians." The HBC built its trading posts around the river outlets along the Hudson's Bay coastline, and sent in the occasional explorer such as Henry Kelsey in 1690 and then Anthony Henday in 1754 to report on the unexplored "Indian Territory".

The Indians became equal partners in the fur trade economy. Both parties benefited from their mutual trade activities, the posts becoming centres of commercial and social activity. Indian families and bands brought furs and fresh meat to exchange for trade goods.

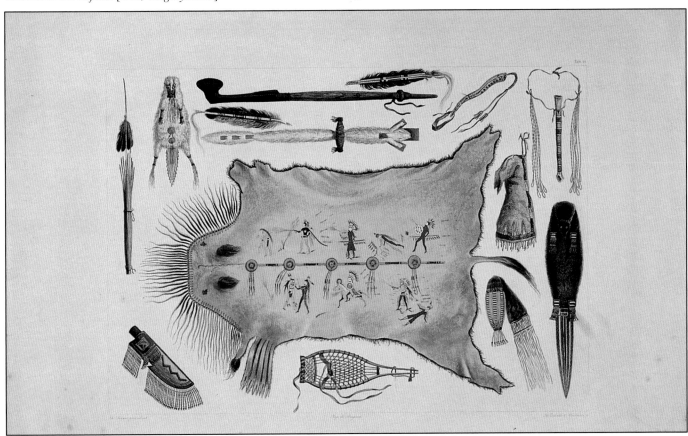

"Indian Utensils and Arms" by Karl Bodmer. This display of artifacts is a fine representation of Plains Indians culture of mid-19th century. The pictographs on the buffalo robe depict major historical events and personal exploits of the owner. Beadwork, porcupine quill work, as well as natural materials [e.g. feathers and bones] ornament the objects. [GM, Calgary/2025]

They gradually adopted more of the white man's food, clothing, and technology, becoming less self-sufficient and instead of producing for their own tribal needs, they now supplied the growing European fur market. The Cree, in particular, enjoyed an unprecedented growth in power and influence as middlemen in the fur trade network. They pushed aside other tribes such as the Sioux. On the Plains they formed alliances with the Ojibway and Assiniboine. They readily adopted weapons that offered more security against starvation, protection from enemies, and a means to obtain luxury trade items. The fur trade had a great impact upon Indian society and on their material culture. The gun replaced the bow and arrow; metal utensils replaced bone, wood, stone and leather artifacts; the kettle augmented pottery; European clothing was preferred to hides; beads were used with seeds, quills and feathers; and manufactured goods augmented traditional foods. By the turn of the 18th century, several bands in northern Manitoba were referred to as "post Indians" largely dependent on the HBC for their needs. Also, the hundreds of European traders gave rise to a new aboriginal race of people — the Métis.

The prairie Indians relied primarily on the plains bison or buffalo which numbered in the tens of millions. Although antelope, deer, elk, and fur bearing animals were alternative sources of sustenance, the buffalo hunt was the most spectacular tribal activity.

1. *"A Buffalo Rift" by A. J. Miller. The buffalo hunt was the most spectacular tribal activity; driving the buffalo over the steep cliffs was one method of killing these prime monarchs. [Public Archives of Canada [PAC]] 2. "Buffalo Meat Drying", Red River 1899; water colour by William Armstrong (1822-1914). [PAC/C-10502]*

1.

They captured the buffalo during the summer in communal hunts, using buffalo pounds (or corrals) or by driving them over steep cliffs (buffalo jumps). Hunters also stalked the buffalo in wolf skins and on horseback. The buffalo provided a year round food source. Delicacies such as buffalo tongues were required for religious feasts such as the Sun Dance. During the height of the fur trade in the 19th century, buffalo meat was dried and mixed with tallow and berries to make pemmican for the fur trade companies. The pemmican trade, and later the sale of hides for industrial use, led to

2.

the buffalo's over-exploitation by mid-century. By the early 1880s the plains bison was extinct. The Indians north of the 49th parallel now called on the Queen's representatives to honour their commitments of economic assistance as promised in the treaties.

Treaties between the Indian Nations and the British in eastern Canada before Confederation in 1867 set the precedent for the "numbered" treaties of the 1870s. Beginning with Treaty No. 1 in 1871 covering southern Manitoba and concluding with Treaty No. 7 in 1877 covering southern Alberta, the federal government obtained legal land cessations in return for various "treaty rights." Indian reserve lands were set aside under Crown trust. Using a formula of one square mile for a family of five (or 128 acres per capita), the government surveyed the reserves. Indian leaders were promised agricultural assistance and economic aid; some were provided an ammunition allowance and fishing twine; schools were built and teachers provided by the department of Indian Affairs in co-operation with the Anglican, Methodist and Roman Catholic churches. The promise of a "medicine chest" in Treaty 6 has been interpreted as meaning free medicare but not free medical facilities.

The many treaty negotiations, each lasting several days and requiring sophisticated language interpretation, have resulted in many legal cases over the years involving land claims. Many of the English concepts with respect to land ownership and legal terminology used in the treaties were not readily translatable into native tongues, giving rise to conflicting claims over the ownership of natural resources. The government has consistently viewed the treaties as final land extinguishments whereas Indian Nations have traditionally argued that they only agreed to share the surface soil and never intentionally surrendered the other resources now under provincial jurisdiction. To the European immigrants, land was a commodity for sale, exploitation or individual possession; to the Indian, land was the source of all life. The air, the sun, the water, and the soil could not be selfishly owned and therefore could never be sold or "surrendered" to the European. Nevertheless, the "White man's law" took effect when the plains tribes took up their reserve lands under the Indian Act, first consolidated in 1876 and still in force today.

The new transcontinental railway, completed in 1885, and the federal government's policy of promoting western settlement, encouraged settlement at the turn of the century of hundreds of thousands of newcomers. Traditional hunting grounds were closed to Indians when national parks were established, beginning with the Rocky Mountain Park (Banff) in 1885. Later provincial parks and wilderness areas further reduced the available unoccupied Crown lands where treaty Indians were guaranteed the right to enjoy their traditional occupations and life style. High mortality rates persisted from smallpox, measles and influenza. Tuberculosis became the great killer on the reserves well into the 1920s. Despite great medical improvements, the native population still continues to suffer the highest mortality rate in Canada.

Once settled on reserves, the Indian population was subjected to concerted efforts by government officials to replace their former hunting economy with agriculture and/or ranching. While the Indian department sought to "civilize" the Indian people through education and an agriculturally based economy, the church sought to "Christianize" them along the same lines. Children were enrolled in industrial and boarding schools, thus separating them from their traditional beliefs and culture. Corporal punishment was administered to students speaking their native language while contact with family members was severely restricted or eliminated. Sacred ceremonies such as the Sun Dance were outlawed under penalty by the Indian Act. Government officials and the Canadian public believed well into the 1930s that the Indian race would never survive and that assimilation was inevitable.

"Sun Dance Scene, Blood Reserve, 1906" by Gerald Tailfeathers. This scene shows three Blood Indians preparing for the "coups counting" activities at a giveaway dance. The Sun Dance is held annually at the traditional campsite at the base of Belly Buttes on the Blood Reserve in southern Alberta. [*GM, Calgary/318 BW*]

In retrospect, the 1920s proved to be a turning point for the prairie tribes as their populations slowly began to rebound and they became more politically assertive. The Ontario based League of Indians of Canada was formed in 1919 by F.O. Loft and within a year he had organized groups in Manitoba and Saskatchewan. Indian leaders passed numerous resolutions calling for religious freedom, better health and education services, asking for the right to travel off their reserves without government passes, demanding that no further land surrenders be undertaken, that economic programs be instituted, and generally, that the spirit and terms of the treaties be honoured and respected. Annual conferences were hosted alternately between Saskatchewan and Alberta bands under the revitalized League of Indians of Western Canada. In both 1939 and 1944, the influential and powerful Federation of Saskatchewan

1. *Indian Affairs Minister Jean Chrétien, in the early 1970s, meeting with Stoney Band Council to discuss land claims. [Photo/W. Getty]* 2. *Chief Johnny Smallboy (1898-1984), of Cree lineage, drew national attention to urban and reserve Indian problems. He "returned to the land" and established a working community used as a retreat by Plains Indians from both the U.S.A. and Western Canada before he died at Smallboy Camp. [Photo/W. Getty]*

1.

2.

Indians and the Indian Association of Alberta were incorporated to continue the fight for changes in the Indian Act and to preserve fundamental treaty rights. The fight for better health services resulted in nursing stations and medical clinics on reserves; schools were upgraded and integrated education in neighbouring towns came to replace the old boarding schools; higher education and job training programs were funded and band councils assumed more responsibility for administration of band services such as housing, roads, social services and other normal municipal services.

In the 1960s Indian band councils and provincial Indian organizations continued to gain credibility, although they still relied on federal trusteeship under ministerial authority. The government's "White Paper" on Indian Policy in 1969 prompted a vehement counter-attack, in particular from the Indian Chiefs of Alberta and

1, 2. *The Canadian Monarchy has always taken an active interest in Canada's native people and native people have constantly been loyal supporters of the Canadian Monarchy. These two illustrations show Queen Elizabeth II and H.R.H. Prince Philip, Duke of Edinburgh, in the 1970s, visiting with their loyal subjects in Calgary.* [*Photo/W. Getty*]

1.

2.

the Manitoba Indian Brotherhood. Indeed, the federal government revised its land claims policies, partially in response to supportive court decisions recognizing aboriginal rights and upholding the federal government's trusteeship relationship with Indian people. The Constitution Act of 1982 recognized the special rights and status of Canada's Indian Nations and other aboriginal groups by providing under Section 35 of the new Charter of Rights and Freedoms that: "The existing aboriginal and treaty rights of the aboriginal peoples of Canada are hereby recognized and affirmed." This clause was included at the last moment after a massive international lobby by Canada's native peoples, and after Canada was reminded by British jurist Lord Denning of her moral duty to honour the treaties. In part, Lord Denning's statement on this moral duty was very emphatic:

> Indians will be able to say that their rights and freedoms have been guaranteed to them by the Crown — originally by the Crown in respect of the United Kingdom — now by the Crown in respect of Canada — but, in any case, by the Crown. No Parliament should do anything to lessen the worth of these guarantees. They should be honoured by the

1. *The family is essential in preserving the heritage of Canada's native people. Here the old and the young, the grandmother with her grandchildren, come together on the ancestral pastures of those who have gone before them.* [*Photo/W. Getty*]

2. *Chief Smallboy's Cree mother, in her mid-90's, preparing to attend meeting to discuss aboriginal rights, ca. 1970.* [*Photo/W. Getty*]

1.

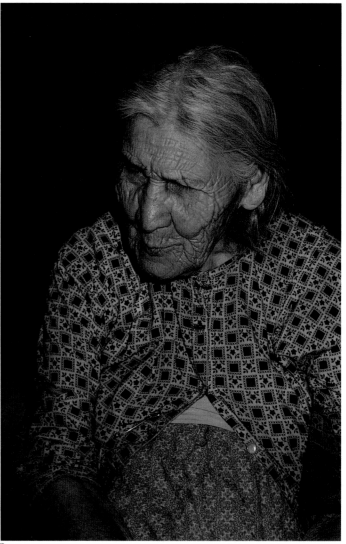

2.

Crown in respect of Canada as long as the sun rises and the river flows. That promise must never be broken.

The recommendations of the Parliamentary Report on Indian Self-government (Penner Report) in 1983 and the on-going constitutional discussions at the First Minister's conferences on identifying native rights have legitimized and strengthened the right of Indian Nations to self-government. In 1985, a new pan-Indian alliance was officially organized as the Prairie Treaty Nations Alliance in order to co-ordinate their efforts in the area of constitutional entreachment of treaty rights, defending land claims and reclaiming control over their own destiny through Indian government. Over 130 Indian bands from Manitoba, Saskatchewan, Alberta, and north-eastern British Columbia today are determined to re-affirm the bi-lateral relationship with the Crown set down in the treaties. As Indian governments, they are demanding a rightful share of income from natural resources, control over band membership (citizenship), and constitutional protection for their special status and rights guaranteed in the treaties. It is evident that the plains Indian Nations of Canada want their constitutional rights recognized in order to continue building solid relationships based upon "peace and friendship" with the Canadian people.

Summer Camp and Pow-Wow. Following the footsteps of their forbears, Plains Indians assemble for their annual pow-wow in the Alberta foothills. [Photo/W. Getty]

Indians of the N.W.T., the Yukon, and the B.C. Interior
Wayne Getty

Stamp: *This Canada Post stamp depicts the Dance of the Kutcha-Kutchin. Natives of the Yukon Region frequently sought out game through ceremonial songs and dancing.*

The Athapaskan speaking native people form the third largest Indian linguistic group within Canada. While a few live in the northern section of the prairie provinces, the vast majority occupy the scarcely populated frontier areas of the Northwest Territories, the Yukon and Northern B.C. The tribal groups of the Athapaskan peoples living in the N.W.T. and now calling themselves the Dene are the Chipewyan, Beaver, Slaveys, Dogrib and Yellowknives of the N.W.T.; the Hare, Kutchin and Nahani of the Yukon; and the Chilcotin, Carrier, Sekani and Tahltan of Northern B.C. The southern interior of B.C. is populated by the tribes of two linguistic groups: the Interior Salish and the Kootenay.

Historically, the cultural patterns of the various Athapaskan tribes were very similar to the extent that tribal groups, separated by over 1000 miles and each with its own particular dialect, could still understand the conversation of other Athapaskan tribes. Similarities existed in their religious practices — such as the seeking of the guardian spirit, the use of medicine men in healing or warding off evil spirits, the burial practice of covering the body with a small

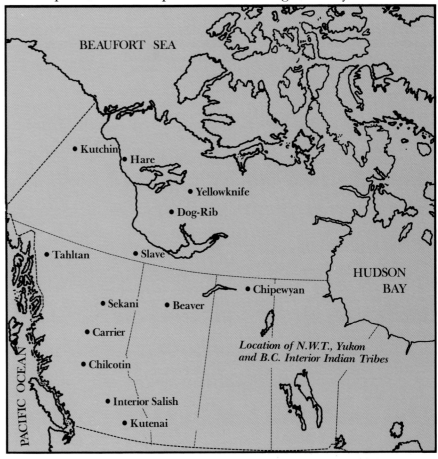

Location of N.W.T., Yukon and B.C. Interior Indian Tribes

1.

hut and placing the property of the deceased with the body to help in the afterlife. The moon, rather than the sun was worshipped by the prairie tribes and was the focus for most of their religious ceremonies. At puberty, young girls went through a period of seclusion while young men fasted in a quest for their guardian spirit.

These tribes were primarily hunting, fishing, and gathering societies which had to be mobile to ensure a plentiful supply of food, especially during the long, harsh winters. Consequently their homes were often not permanent structures. During the summer they constructed huts of poles or simple lean-tos covered with brush; in winter, they used tipis covered with hides. Their tools were very basic and included such items as stone adzes and knives, chisels of antlers and beaver teeth, hooks and awls of bone. Weapons were the spear, the bow and arrow, sinew snares, and willow bark nets. They also used willow to make water-tight baskets while dishes were constructed from wood and bark. Most of the tribes used toboggans,

1. Athapaskan burial ground in Whitehorse, Yukon. Athapaskans, at time of burial, traditionally cover the body with a small hut. [Photo/Gayle Jenkins] 2. Skin Lodges of the Dogribs in front of the Hudson's Bay Fort at Great Slave Lake, ca. 1900. [Morris Norman] 3. Athapaskan natives such as this one, ca. 1910, have supplemented their income since the mid-19th century by acting as hunt guides. [C.J. Humber] 4. Athapaskan tipi, constructed in traditional fashion from pine or spruce, ca. 1965. [Photo/Wayne Getty]

2.

3.

4.

1.

2.

1. Athapaskan clothing was made from prepared skins. The native in view is scraping, stretching and drying a moosehide near Atlin, B.C., ca. 1900. [C.J. Humber] 2. Like the Algonkian tribes of eastern Canada, the Northwest Territories and Yukon Indians have traditionally resorted to the birchbark canoe for transportation. Here Slavey Indians prepare to trade at Fort Resolution, ca. 1900. 3. This Canada Post Corporation stamp depicts a Kutchin Indian of the Athapaskan peoples ready for the hunt.

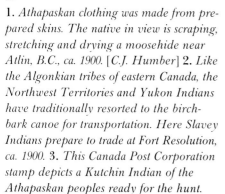

3.

but a few also used the sled as developed by the Eskimo. The extensive waterways of the north resulted in the use of birch bark canoes as the principal method of transportation. Some tribes also used dogs as pack animals.

Covering materials for warmth and protection were made primarily from prepared skins with the caribou being a major source of both food and hides for the northern groups while the buffalo was the major source for southern groups. Clothing was a simple loose fitting shirt or dress with the added use of a fur robe for warmth in the winter. In addition, most tribes used caps or hoods, mittens, leggings, and moccasins.

Tattooing, along with face and body painting, were the primary means of personal ornamentation; however clothing was decorated by using porcupine quill and moose hair embroidery with beaver and rabbit fur serving as trim. Tattooing was done by puncturing skin with an awl and then drawing a sinew thread, covered with charcoal, through the puncture. A few tribes used a red pigment instead of black charcoal. Headbands and necklaces were sometimes embroidered but more frequently were made of claws, teeth, bone and antler.

The focus of social life was the extended family with the tribes being divided into exogamous clans which ensured that marriage would occur outside the close family. Hunting and war leaders were chosen on the basis of demonstrated wisdom and courage, but the position appears to have had no tribal authority outside of the particular action for which the leader was chosen. Warfare was frequent between neighbouring tribes; and, while the southern groups made slaves of their captives, having a well established system of nobles, commoners and slaves, the northern groups usually took no captives and appear to have had no strong social status grouping other than those based on sex and age differences.

1.

In general, the Athapaskan tribes shared a common woodlands culture; however, those living in the northern parts adapted elements of Eskimo culture while those in the south and near the coast adapted elements of either the coastal or plains cultures. The basic reality of life was that these people lived in a harsh land where their existence depended upon the whims of nature. Extremes varied from the long warm days of summer to the bitter cold nights of winter, from abundance of vast caribou or buffalo herds to the virtual disappearance of game. These people had little control over their survival from season to season, from year to year, yet their populations appear to have been stable until smallpox epidemics decimated them during the 19th and early 20th century.

In south-central B.C. both the Interior Salish and the Kootenay were primarily fishing and gathering societies whose cultural patterns reflected an adaptation of a few elements from the coastal tribes but many more elements from the plains tribes. The Interior Salish, the largest tribe in central B.C. numbering over 15,000 in

2.

1. *The cultural influence of the Northwest Coast Indians is visible in this view as Athapaskans from Carcross, Yukon, ca. 1920, prepare for a potlatch dance.* [*C.J. Humber*]
2. *Interior British Columbia native peoples, such as this Salish woman, above, and the Salish chief, below, show the influence of the Plains Indians in their dress.* [*Public Archives of Canada* [*PAC*]]
3. *During the summer, interior natives of British Columbia assembled for annual pow wows. Here a Thompson River group pose for this ca. 1900 photograph by Maynard.* [*PAC*]

3.

4.

1800 according to J. Mooney as published in *Aboriginal Population of America*, did not have the clan system or secret societies of the coastal Salish. The band foundation was the extended family with a chieftainship that was passed on to the eldest son; however, the chief's role was limited and real authority lay with a council of elders. The Salish were renowned as an aggressive people who fought, not just outside groups, but even against other Salish tribes. In general, only women and children were taken as captives but they were not kept as slaves but integrated into the tribe by either marriage or adoption. Marriage occurred within the band thus serving to strengthen family bonds through blood ties.

While these tribes did have an area they controlled, they were a relatively sedentary group. Winter homes were permanent, semi-subterranean circular structures made of logs and covered with earth. The summer residence was an easily constructed conical hut covered with rush mats. Their principal food source was salmon, but they also hunted land mammals and gathered a variety of roots and berries. Birch bark was used to make some household vessels and canoes, but these people were renowned for their tightly woven baskets, decorated by a process known as imbrication. Summer transportation was the birch bark canoe. A few bands made dug-out canoes, but in the winter they used snow-shoes and toboggans. Dogs were widely used as pack animals all year round.

Religious activities were similar to those of the Plains Indians. Sweat lodges were used for both purification and healing rituals with the Ghost Dance being their major religious practice. At puberty young women went into a period of seclusion that could last for up to four years and similarly young men isolated themselves in a search for their guardian spirit.

The Kootenay lived on the eastern slopes of the Rockies until the early part of the 18th century when they were driven westward into B.C. by the Blackfoot and Stoney tribes. Here their territory covered south eastern B.C. and down into Idaho. Cultural patterns still strongly resembled those of the plains tribes, and up until the latter part of the 19th century, they regularly crossed back to the prairies to trade at Rocky Mountain House and Bow Fort and to hunt the buffalo in the foothills. Clothing was made from skins and their homes were tipis covered with buffalo hides or rush mats. Like the Salish they used birch bark for utensils and canoes. Ornamentation consisted of realistic figures painted on tents, garments and their bodies and some tattooing was practised by both males and females.

Band organization was built around the extended family with each band having a hereditary chief supported by a council of

1. The Monarchs of the Plain, ca. 1900. The Kootenay, living on the eastern slopes of the Rockies, frequently returned to the prairies to hunt buffalo, the sustenance of their forebears. [Robert Wilson] 2. Mrs. Ambrose Gravelle, Kootenay Indian, with her twin daughters in decorated cradle boards, ca. 1920. [Glenbow Archives [GA], Calgary]

1.

2.

elders. The Blackfoot and Stoney were their traditional enemy and the Salish became enemies after their move into B.C. Warfare was continuous with captured women and children being rapidly integrated into the tribe as brave warriors were expected to have more than one wife. The focus of religious worship was the sun with sweat lodges being used extensively in religious and healing activities. Medicine men played an important role in both spiritual rituals and physical healing with the use of herbs and traditional "medicines". All adolescent males and females had to acquire a guardian spirit and this was done in the form of a dream quest carried out while fasting in seclusion.

1. Raising poles for Kootenay Sun Dance lodge with medicine man in nest, ca. 1920. [GA, Calgary] 2. Upper Kootenay Indians, with child in horse travois, at David Thompson Memorial Celebration, Lake Windermere, B.C., 1922. [GA, Calgary] 3. An Edward S. Curtis haunting photograph of a Kootenay girl, ca. 1910. [GA, Calgary]

1.

2.

This area of the interior of B.C. extending into the Yukon and the N.W.T. was the last of the pioneer frontier. White settlement was well established on both the coast and the prairies before these tribes came under pressures from white expansion largely caused by mineral resource exploration and development.

The establishment of trading posts throughout the northern areas during the middle of the 19th century did attract isolated bands as they sought to acquire trade goods such as metal axes, beads, blankets and clothing materials. While a few bands did establish permanent settlements near the trading posts, most groups adhered to their traditional lands and way of life and had only occasional contact with the white man. On the heals of the entrepreneurs came missionaries, often following the bands to the hinterlands to build churches and schools, the result of which was the creation of various Indian village settlements.

By the latter part of the 19th century, most tribes had been brought under the direct influence of the federal government whose stated policy was to confine Indians within village areas so that children could be "civilized" by "conversion to Christianity" and

3.

educated in church operated schools. This concentration of the Indian people encouraged the spread of smallpox which decimated the native populations. Mooney estimates that by the turn of the 19th century all of these northern tribes had lost somewhere between one-half to three-quarters of their population as compared to the previous century.

1.   2.

1. *Converted to Christianity, interior British Columbia native peoples established communities and built churches such as this Roman Catholic one in Lillooet, B.C., ca. 1910. [C.J. Humber]* 2. *British Columbia natives frequently built villages near larger towns such as this one at Mount Paul, near Kamloops, ca. 1910. [C.J. Humber]*

A few in the N.W.T. signed Treaty No. 8 in 1899; however, the greater part of the territories was covered by the signing of Treaty No. 11 in 1921, only after oil was found at Norman Wells and the government wanted to ensure control of oil producing lands. To date several terms of this treaty have not been fulfilled, one being that reserve lands (one square mile per family of five) have never been set aside for the Indians in the N.W.T. On the other hand, the Indians in B.C. and the Yukon have never signed a treaty with the federal government. For most bands, however, land has been set aside for Indian use and these lands have a legal status similar to that of treaty reserves.

The natives of B.C. and the Yukon are status Indians, who can claim full aboriginal rights and have been granted "native" rights under the Indian Act, but have not been given all of the specific rights guaranteed to Indians who have signed treaties. This distinction between "status" Indians — who are recognized legally as Indians even though they have not signed any treaty — and "treaty"' Indians — who have given up oboriginal rights and claims in exchange for rights and compensation as specified in the treaty they signed — is important as it means that "status" Indians are in a position to negotiate the terms and conditions of any treaty they sign in a contemporary context with reference to today's needs, values and standard of living. On the other hand "treaty" Indians can only dispute the legality of a treaty and negotiate as to the specific meaning of the various clauses and whether the federal government has fulfilled its obligations under the terms of that treaty.

The federal government's stated policy of confining Indians to reserve lands and their subsequent conversion and subjugation through the activities of both church and school has inevitably resulted in the disintegration of many traditional activities, beliefs and practices. This cultural dislocation and decline has been a major contributor to the social problems prevalent on so many reserves today. In retrospect, it is easy to condemn the policies of both church and state. Given the beliefs and knowledge of European cultures at that time, however, the people involved in both forming and implementing policy acted out of a sincere belief in what they thought was for the good of the Indians and the betterment of Canada.

Because of their relative isolation and the lack of significant white settlement in the area, the natives in northern B.C., the Yukon and the N.W.T. were able to hold to traditional patterns for several decades after other tribes in the south had changed; but, "civilization" did catch up to them by the turn of the century. In 1896, two Athapaskan Indians, Shookum Jim and Tagish Charlie, along with George Cormack, found gold on Bonanza Creek near Dawson City in the Yukon. The gold rush was on, and, by 1899, the Yukon had a larger population than any of the prairie provinces and Dawson City, with a population of over 25,000, was the largest city west of Winnipeg. During this boom, native people served as guides for many of the white prospectors, frequently saving the lives of these northern novices, but rarely participating directly in the search for wealth. By 1910, the dream was over and the country reverted to the Indians. Even though over $100 million in gold had been taken out, only a very few natives shared in this prosperity but all native lives were forevermore changed. The Yukon gold rush not only exposed native people to contact with large numbers of whites who used and abused them, but also it left them with a legacy of government bureaucracy, policy control, a taste of city life, and a large number of half-breed children.

In reaction to pressure from the churches, the government made most native religious practices and ceremonies illegal. New weapons, tools, clothing and food were introduced through trading posts, prospectors, missionaries and the government. As the Indians' material culture changed they became more and more dependent upon the white man's culture and moved into settlements where they would have easier access to the technology. Some bands still lived in the hinterland and the bush, but those who moved into settlements found that part of the process of "properly" educating natives meant that children were taken from their families and placed in mission boarding schools. Here they were generally forbidden to speak their own language, were not allowed to practise traditional

Skookum Jim and Tagish Charlie, Athapaskan natives from the Yukon, helped begin the rush to the Yukon in 1898 by finding gold on Bonanza Creek near Dawson City, pictured here, ca. 1900, the largest city west of Winnipeg by 1899. [Robert Wilson]

cultural activities, were limited in their contact with their families and in general were taught a white man's culture which had little or no practical applicability within their own environment.

World War II and the construction of the Alaska Highway brought another large influx of outsiders, this time over 30,000 U.S. soldiers and with them, lots of money. When the army left after four years, native people were understandably reluctant to give up the ma-

1.

1. *The salmon run in rivers is important for Canada's native people. After being trapped in fish weirs, salmon are dried in the sun for winter consumption. View is along the Yukon River, near Whitehorse, 1961. [Photo/Gayle Jenkins]* **2.** *A group of Dogrib Indian boys, ca. 1900, on Great Slave Lake. [C.J. Humber]*

2.

terialistic culture and easier lifestyle to which they had grown accustomed in the towns; however, there were no more jobs and no more money. Seizing an opportunity to establish stronger control over the native population, Indian Affairs stepped in with welfare, membership registration, housing and other enticements to keep the Indians out of the bush. In reality, these paternalistic actions served only to accelerate the pattern of social disintegration; within a few years natives were faced with large scale problems related to alcohol abuse, poor housing and nutrition, poverty, crime and ill health.

In the N.W.T., a similar pattern of cultural and social decay evolved as mineral resource development drew more and more whites into the north country. Even though most natives were excluded from direct participation in or benefits from such developments, like the Yukon Indians they were lured from their traditional "way of life" and into settlements under the control of church and state.

Throughout the north, even though natives were the majority population, they were excluded by law from participating in the political processes up until the 1960s. But change was around the corner. Young people were getting educated. More importantly, native people questioned the inequities they encountered and demanded justice and control over their own lives. Native people organized themselves, and even though they often lacked adequate funds, they started to research problems, to propose alternatives and to pressure the federal government to include natives in government decision making processes.

In 1973, the Council For Yukon Indians, led by Chief Elijah Smith, presented a proposal to Prime Minister Trudeau for a treaty and land claims settlement entitled "Together Today For Our Chil-

1. *Harold Cardinal, a Woodland Indian, author and important spokesman for the Dene, a significant grouping of Athapaskan Indians, attending a 1969 conference on Indian rights. [Photo/Wayne Getty]* 2. *Yukon Native Women in the 1970s attending a conference on native women's rights in Whitehorse. [Photo/Wayne Getty]* 3. *"Indian Rights for Indian Women", a badge worn by Indian women pursuing their native rights in the 1970s. [C.J. Humber]*

1.

2.

3.

1.

2.   3.

1. *Cover of presentation paper, about treaty and land claims settlement, made by Yukon Indians to the Canadian Prime Minister in 1973.* [*Council for Yukon Indians* [*CYI*]] 2. *Chief Elijah Smith, Yukon Indian, a major native leader for Indian rights and land claims in the Yukon.* [*CYI*] 3. *The Hon. Margaret Joe, native Athapaskan, is the Minister of Health and Human Resources for the current Yukon government, whose policy is supportive of Indian land claims. She is also the minister responsible for the Women's Directorate.* [*CYI*]

dren Tomorrow." This was the first time in Canadian history that any native group had spelled out what it thought would be a fair settlement for the extinguishment of its aboriginal rights and land claims. These people were visionaries. They were not concerned with how much they would get today. Instead, they laid out a plan which would ensure that native people would be an integral part of the Yukon by establishing a sound economic and social base which would enhance their cultural identity "for our children tomorrow".

While this proposal was initially greeted with enthusiasm and indications of acceptability by the federal government, meaningful negotiations have led nowhere as Ottawa is apparently resistant to any creative innovations deviating from the traditional patterns of treaty settlements. Much of this resistance was generated by a non-native population pressuring the Yukon Government to oppose the plan put forward by the C.Y.I. This may change with the 1985 election of a new government whose policy is supportive of Indian land claims and in which there are now two natives, Margaret Joe, Minister of Health and Human Resources, and David Porter, Minister of Tourism and Renewable Resources, as members of cabinet.

Similar aspirations were generated in the N.W.T., and culminated in the native people's response to the proposal to build the MacKenzie Pipeline. In the face of the threat to their culture and their land, native people organized to oppose the construction of any pipeline before land claims were settled, thereby ensuring that land vital to native interests would not be damaged. The federal government appointed the Berger Inquiry to investigate and to make recommendations as to the impact such construction would have upon the environment and the people of the north country. The Berger inquiry and report led to putting the proposed development on indefinite hold; of greater importance was the face that native people — the Inuit, the Treaty Indians and the Métis who had worked together — now realized that they could influence government decisions.

In the summer of 1975 under the leadership of James Wah-Shee, a Dogrib Indian from Fort Rae, the natives of the N.W.T. met at Fort Simpson and issued their declaration on the Dene Nation which asserts their "right to self-determination as a distinct people and the recognition of the Dene Nation." This is a historic document in that it proposes to establish an independent Dene Nation within the confederation of Canada, through which native people could exercise self-determination and have total control over their own affairs. An agreement in principle has been reached on the Dene Declaration and the federal government is in the process of finalizing an agreement by which the N.W.T. will be divided into autonomous areas within which native people will have control. In these areas they will have an opportunity to put into practise the basic principles and ideas they feel are necessary to maintain their cultural identity and integrity. In the N.W.T., native people are politicized and many have run successfully for office. Today, Nick Sibbeston, a Metis from Fort Simpson who was the first native northerner to become a lawyer, is the current government leader, while Tagah Curley is the Minister for Energy, Mines and Resources. Other natives, including James Wah-Shee, sit as members of the legislature.

In south-central B.C. native people have been in intense contact with the white population for over a hundred years. Many of the reserves are located close to towns and cities; many Indians have adapted quite well to the changes of contemporary Canadian society. Since the early 1970s most bands have taken control of their own affairs through local self-government and have established cultural, educational and economic development programs for their people. In the late 1960s, Len Marchand, M.P. from the Okanagan, was the first Indian elected as a Member of Parliament.

Social problems still exist, but natives are taking responsibility for solving these problems and identifying the direction of change and the goals for the future. The settlement of aboriginal rights and resulting land claims remains a major problem which both the federal and provincial governments are neglecting to negotiate in any meaningful manner.

Native people have demonstrated that they are patient and long suffering but how long will they be willing to deal with what they perceive as a brick wall before deciding to tear it down...

A people who were doomed for extinction a century ago have, like Lazarus in the Bible, been resurrected and are becoming a significant force within the Canadian mosaic.

1.

2.

1. *The Hon. Nick Sibbetson, a Metis from Fort Simpson and the first native northerner to become a lawyer, is the current government leader in the North West Territories.* [*Government of the N.W.T.*] 2. *The Hon. Tagah Curley is the former Minister for Energy, Mines and Resources in the N.W.T. He reflects the desire of sub-arctic native people who want direct involvement in policies affecting status and non-status Indians.* [*Government of the N.W.T.*]

The Pangnirtung Pass which runs through Auyuittuk National Park on Baffin Island. Its soaring mountains have only recently been discovered by climbers; its rugged beauty has been revered for centuries by the Inuit. [Dept. of Regional and Industial Expansion]

Stamp: *Indians called the Inuit, Eskimos, which in Algonkian language means "raw meat eaters". The view here is a soapstone carving of an Inuit seal harpooning. [Canada Post Corporation]*

The Inuit of Canada
Ian Creery

Those who have not visited the Arctic perhaps imagine it as a vast, featureless desert of rock and ice. At over two million square kilometres, it is certainly immense, but there is much diversity in the Arctic landscape. It includes the verdant hills and sandy beaches of Bathurst Inlet, the glaciers and towering mountains of Baffin Island, and the rolling tundra of the Keewatin. It supports a healthy plant and animal life, and hosts the summer migration of millions of birds. It is also the home of a remarkable people: the Inuit, or Eskimos. The word *eskimo* comes from a Cree Indian word, *aski-mowew*, which means "he eats it raw". Nowadays, they prefer to be called Inuit, which in their language means 'the people'. There are about 100,000 Inuit in the circumpolar world — 25,000 in Canada, 42,000 in Greenland, 31,500 in Alaska, and 1,500 in Siberia. Most of Canada's Inuit live in the Northwest Territories, and the rest live along the coasts of Northern Quebec and Labrador.

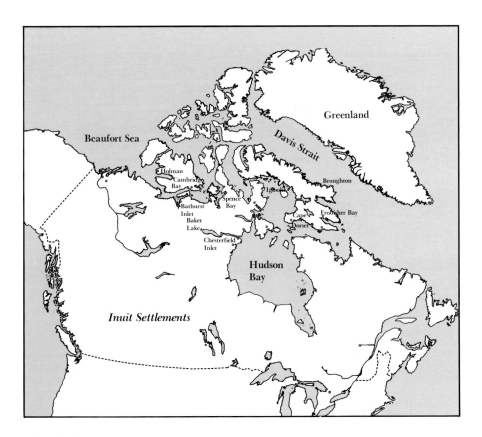

Inuit Settlements

1.

1. *The huge bowhead whale was a steady source of food for the Inuit until the cooling of the climate, about 1200 A.D., made this mammal scarce.* [*Canada Post Corporation*]
2. *N.W.T. Inuit family in large leather boat, 1897, on hunting and fishing expedition.* [*Geological Survey of Canada, Ottawa*]
3. *Kayaks, 16 feet long and covered with sealskin, were used by Canada's arctic Inuit to hunt the seal, a staple food for centuries.* [*Morris Norman*]

2.

3.

Origins

No one has established positively how the Inuit came to North America. What seems likely, though, is that their ancestors arrived at the tail end of the migration of Indian peoples across the Bering land bridge from Siberia to Alaska about 10,000 B.C. Over the next 8,000 years a culture evolved, probably in Alaska, which adapted winter clothing and hunting techniques to cope with the harsh Arctic conditions. Starting in 2000 B.C., this group, followed by later ones, populated the Arctic from Alaska to Greenland, living in small camps that were often wiped out by starvation.

In 1000 A.D. a new wave of migrants, known as the Thule culture, came from Alaska to spread across the whole Arctic. They had developed large harpoon heads and floats to hunt the huge bowhead whale. This steady source of food enabled them to thrive where others had starved. They were the direct ancestors of today's Inuit. About 1200 A.D., a cooling in the climate led to the disappearance of the bowhead from many areas, and Inuit who had depended on it were forced to look for other sources of food. Their adaptations broke the previously uniform Inuit culture into nine regional cultures which developed some substantial differences between one another. For instance, while the Mackenzie Inuit in the west continued living in large camps and depended on the whale for survival, the North Baffin Inuit lived on walrus, caribou and seal, forsaking the traditional sod house for snowhouses in winter and skin tents in other seasons.

The most successful groups hunted a wide variety of animals, moving from place to place as the seasons dictated. Most of their time was spent by the sea, hunting whale and walrus in the autumn and seal in the winter, but they would make inland journeys to hunt caribou, which provided food and skins for warm winter clothing. The Inuit would also travel to inland fishing lakes, and would stalk the migrating ducks and geese in spring. Some of their hunting techniques were ingenious: they built converging lines of stone figures, *inukshuks*, to drive caribou into concealed traps, and mimicked seals basking on the sea-ice in springtime, in order to creep close enough to harpoon them.

Although game was sometimes abundant, starvation was always a possibility. Small groups stood a better chance of survival than large ones. Most Inuit lived in camps of two or three related families, who might get together with others once or twice a year at fishing or sealing camps. They placed great value on kinship; many families would adopt a child from another to strengthen the bonds between them. It was also important to share food and possessions: some groups had a distribution system in which each hunter would parcel out his catch to relatives according to a strict formula. An abundant harvest was the occasion of feasting and games. Hunters would dance to the beat of a drum and compose songs about their exploits:

1.

2.

1. *Taken ca. 1900, this Yukon Inuit family stands beside a hide and skin dwelling. The man holds a knife used for cutting snow blocks for a winter home.* [*Morris Norman*]
2. *Taken by the great Canadian arctic explorer, A.P. Low, this photo shows an Inuit family standing beside their skin tent near Fort Chimo, Quebec in 1896.* [*Public Archives of Canada* [*PAC*]/*C-5591*]

Glorious it is to see
The caribou flocking down from the forests
And beginning
Their wanderings to the north.
Timidly they watch
For the pitfalls of man.

All in all, the Inuit lived a precarious existence. They were acutely aware of natural and supernatural forces they could not control. Their religion was shamanism, characterized succinctly by

The following numbered stamps appear:

1. CANADA · POSTES · POSTAGE · CARIBOU · 4

2. Canada 12 — Inuit-Hunting Les Inuits-La chasse

3. Canada 17 — Inuit-Community Les Inuit-La communauté

4. Canada 17 — Inuit-Community Les Inuit-La communauté

5. Canada 35 — Inuit-Spirits Les Inuits-Le surnaturel

6. Canada 17 — Inuit-Spirits Les Inuits-Le surnaturel

the Igloolik shaman Aua: "We do not believe, we fear…" The shamans were a combination of mystic and magician, treating sickness and advising on hunting problems with the help of sleight-of-hand and a system of taboos. They mediated between their fellow men and the world of such spirits as the goddess Taleelayo, who lived at the bottom of the sea.

The Inuit did not live a comfortable life, but they were familiar with their world and confident in their ability to cope with difficulties. However, their world was changing: the climate was cooling, game was harder to find, the danger of starvation was increasing. In addition, they were facing an even greater challenge: the coming of the white man.

1-6. *A collage of stamps depicting Inuit livelihood: hunting, gaming, printing and sculpting.* [*The Canada Post Corporation*] 7. *Contemporary view of mother and child of the inland caribou people* [*Padlermuit*] *north of Manitoba.* [*PAC/PA-114718*] 8. *The shawl is commonly used to carry babies in the western arctic whereas Inuit from eastern Canada transport their young in the enlarged hood of their parka.* [*PAC/PA-135920*] 9. *Inuit hunter of the Boothia Peninsula, ca. 1950. Goggles carved of bone helped prevent snow blindness.* [*PAC/PA-114680*]

7.

8.

9.

Colonization

The Vikings led by Erik the Red may well have run into Inuit on their voyages to the shores of North America, but most Inuit communities would not have seen their first white man until the European explorers of the 19th century went looking for the Northwest Passage. The explorers traded with the Inuit occasionally, but otherwise showed little interest in them.

The first sustained contact came as Scottish and American whalers appeared regularly during the 19th century, eventually wintering on the east coast of Baffin Island and on the coastline of the Beaufort Sea. Some took Inuit wives. The captains would often hire Inuit to act as guides and crew. The whalers worked themselves out of a job by almost wiping out the bowhead whale, and by the turn of the 20th century had sailed back to Peterhead and Boston.

The whalers were followed by the fur traders, who set up shop in tiny posts all over the Arctic. They traded guns, flour and tea to the Inuit in exchange for fox and wolf furs. These valuable trade goods induced the Inuit to forsake traditional hunting techniques

1. Inuit family of western arctic, ca. 1900. Note the bone ornaments piercing the man's lips. Snow knife is held by the visitor. [Morris Norman] **2.** *Inuit visiting Fort Magnesia, Cape Sabine, Ellesmere Island, ca. 1900. By the turn of the century, Inuit in the far reaches of the arctic were making contact with the whiteman's civilization. [C.J. Humber]* **3.** *Inuit hunter strikes a typical bargain with the trader: fox furs for flour, tea and tobacco. Note studded leather belt around his caribou-skin parka. [PAC/ PA-129942]*

1.

2.

3.

in favour of trapping. They came to depend on high prices offered by the fur markets of the outside world. When fur prices collapsed in the 1940s, the Inuit were left stranded, unable to return to the old ways and without a source of income for trade goods. Many camps suffered a serious lack of food and fell prey to white man's diseases. In the early 1950s some inland Inuit starved to death when the caribou on which they depended failed to appear. Their sorry condition spurred the Canadian government to take up a responsibility it had long neglected.

Government

The Canadian government had never shown much interest in either the Inuit or their land. In the early 1900s, it set up police posts in the Arctic, largely to protect Canadian sovereignty. It was content to leave the welfare of the Inuit to the traders, policemen and missionaries. Louis St. Laurent, Prime Minister from 1948 to 1957, summed it up pretty well: "Apparently we have administered the vast territories of the north in a continuous state of absence of mind."

All changed when Canadians were made aware of the plight of Inuit suffering from the collapse of the fur trade. St. Laurent's government sent relief supplies to the starving, and encouraged Inuit to move to settlements built around the trading posts. It built housing and schools, improved health care, and set up community

A sunny spring day on Broughton Island. Long after the snow has melted from the land, the sea ice remains firm and is used for snowmobile travel. [Photo/Ian Creery]

councils to encourage the growth of local government. In the space of a single decade, the 1950s, nearly all of Canada's Inuit gave up their age-old nomadic way of life to become village dwellers. It was a difficult transition. The necessities of life were now assured, but traditional food was hard to obtain. People used to living in skin tents and igloos had to settle in houses with bedrooms, electric lights and bathtubs. Camps of two or three families were assimilated into settlements of 50 families or more, from different cultural groups. The Inuit were now subject to the rules and regulations of a benevolent but paternalistic government. Could Inuit culture survive?

Transition

The 1960s was also a difficult decade for the Inuit. Following upon the physical changes in their way of life, they had to contend with a government policy which stated that their future lay in assimilating into the Canadian mainstream as fast as possible. The government induced Inuit men to train as miners, cooks and mechanics while their wives took lessons in homemaking, and the children learned to speak English in schools run by southern teachers. The mechanized world of the south was moving north too, in the form of airplanes and skidoos. In 1968 oil was discovered in Alaska, and soon there was a rush of exploration crews into the Canadian Arctic as well.

Faced with the loss of their land and culture, the Inuit fought back. In 1969 the people of the Western Arctic formed COPE, the Committee for Original Peoples Entitlement. COPE was followed two years later by the creation of the ITC, or Inuit Tapirisat of Canada, to represent all of Canada's Inuit. Meanwhile the Inuit of Northern Quebec were organizing to oppose the massive James

A contemporary view of an Inuit hunter departing on a spring hunt. The snow machine's cowling has been removed so the engine won't overheat. [Photo/Jerry Guiberson]

Bay hydroelectric project that threatened to swamp parts of their hunting lands. These groups all wanted to make settlements of their land claims with the Canadian government, in order to protect their way of life while allowing the government to develop the land in ways agreed upon. In 1973 the Northern Quebec Inuit agreed to a land claims settlement with the governments of Quebec and Canada. In 1978 COPE followed suit, signing an agreement covering the western part of the Northwest Territories with the Canadian government. The ITC is still negotiating a claim involving the remaining Inuit land in the N.W.T. ....The government has agreed, however, eventually to divide the N.W.T. in two, the part above the treeline to become Nunavut, or 'our land' in the Inuit language. Nunavut would have an Inuit majority of about 75 percent of its population, thus ensuring a government responsive to Inuit interests.

The settlement today

Just one generation removed from their nomadic life, today's Inuit live in some 46 communities widely scattered across the Arctic. Each region has a bustling centre, like Kuujjuak in Northern Quebec or Cambridge Bay in the Central Arctic, with direct air links to the South. But it is in smaller settlements, such as Repulse Bay or Grise Fiord, perched on rocks by the sea, that the rhythm of life is more balanced between old and new.

Moonlight over Spence Bay, N.W.T. in August. The pack ice has retreated from the bay, but waits on the horizon to recapture the town. [Photo/Ian Creery]

Women who were born in mid-winter igloos on the sea-ice now go to the local nursing station to have their babies. The infant mortality rate is down; the birth rate is up, to two or three times the national average. In fact, the government has trouble supplying enough housing to keep up with this mini population boom. Modern four-bedroom and five-bedroom houses have replaced the one-room shacks that were originally built to take in the first village dwellers, but they are still overcrowded. Many settlements have well-stocked stores, run by the Hudson's Bay Company or local co-ops, which tend to be like oldtime general stores — grocers, clothing, and hardware merchants all rolled into one.

Fresh vegetables and fruit are often available in even the most remote settlements. But many Inuit could not do without their traditional foods: seal, walrus and caribou meat, all eaten raw, frozen, or cooked; lake trout and Arctic char, which closely resembles salmon; ducks and geese, whale skin (called *muktuk*), seaweed and berries in season; rabbits and ptarmigan (like grouse); and many other products of the land. Particularly in smaller settlements, food of the land comprises over 50 percent of the diet. This is a problem for the hunter since hunting does not pay. The cost of equipment and supplies is high, the return low. The meat the hunter gets is valuable to his family but has no commercial worth. When the fur markets pay well, the income covers part of the expense of hunting,

Summer's night sky over Rankin Inlet. North of 60 during the brief arctic summer night is really a short twilight. [*Photo/Ian Creery*]

but the recent European boycott of seal skins has put many hunters on the welfare rolls.

A possible solution to the hunters' economic problem was recommended by former Justice Thomas Berger in his report on northern development in 1977: "Native people consider renewable resources, particularly fur, fish, game and timber, to be essential to their way of life. These resources must be the cornerstone of native economic development." The Canadian government has appeared to neglect this alternative in favour of encouraging Inuit to enter the wage economy. It has spent a lot of money training hunters to work in the oil, gas, and mineral industries, but without much success. There are relatively few jobs available, and many hunters have had trouble adapting to a '9-to-5' mentality so alien to their way of life. Younger Inuit are employed by the government which is arguably the biggest industry in the North, but there are still not enough jobs for those who are now coming out of school. Unemployment in some communities is over 50 percent, and attendant problems such as alcohol and drug abuse have arisen. Family violence has also increased, as older Inuit cope with the dislocation of their lives and the gradual erosion of their culture.

Inuit culture recovers

Since finding their feet in the new settlements, the Inuit have made efforts to understand the source of their problems, and to tackle them before they get out of hand. Many communities have restricted the supply of alcohol until people learn how to deal with its effects. For instance, the town of Frobisher Bay had a severe alcohol problem until local Inuit succeeded in closing the liquor store. Alcohol is still available, but in smaller quantities; many families are happier for the change.

The Inuit have put even greater efforts into halting the erosion

An Inuit camera crew documents a seal hunt. The Inuit Broadcasting Corporation now produces about five hours of television programs a week in the Inuktituk language. [Photo/Jerry Guiberson]

of their culture. They have demanded changes to the school system, which was originally established in the 1960s on a southern model, complete with Dick and Jane readers and teachers from Saskatchewan and Newfoundland. A generation of Inuit schoolchildren grew up who could not properly speak either English or their own language, Inuktitut. The problems of this "lost generation" taught Inuit parents and educators the value of education grounded in the cultural realities of life in the North. The N.W.T. Department of Education now trains Inuit teachers who are gradually replacing southern ones. The children are taught in Inuktitut in the lower grades, and they read about seals and ptarmigan instead of Dick and Jane and dogs called Spot. But many parents want their children to be qualified for office jobs when they leave school; the systems' main challenge is to provide a hybrid Inuit-English education to satisfy all.

The Inuit community's focus on culture and education has also served to modernize Inuktitut. It was only a spoken language until the first missionaries arrived in the North. They adapted two writing systems, one syllabics and the other Roman orthography, for use in translating the Bible into Inuktitut. Only since the 1970s, however, have the two systems come into extensive use in schools and offices. Inuit educators and interpreters have wrestled to adapt the ancient language to the demands of a technological world, and with some ingenuity. Thus, "computer" has been translated as *qaritannguaq*, which means "model of a brain." This renewed interest in Inuktitut has also led to the reclamation of dialects, notably in the Western Arctic, which were in danger of being lost. At the same time, however, as Inuktitut radio broadcasts spread across the North, local dialects are tending to evolve into a standard Inuktitut. These are all signs of a strength that the language will need to hold its own against English.

The future

It appears that, as opposed to many other aboriginal cultures, the Inuit culture will survive. The Inuit now have the political clout to ensure that their language and culture will be protected as they come to terms with Western society. They have also sought help from other countries. The Inuit Circumpolar Conference, created in 1977, brings together Inuit from Alaska, Canada, and Greenland. They have extended a permanent invitation to the Soviet Inuit to join them, should their country allow it. The ICC hopes to promote Inuit interests in the three member countries through social and economic programs, and a common policy on the circumpolar environment.

1.

2.

1. *Artist Kenojuak Ashevak, an Inuit from the West Baffin Eskimo Cooperative at Cape Dorset, N.W.T., is worldwide known for her prints and sculptures.* [*PAC/PA-140297*]
2. *Original drawing for the print "The Owl", 1969, by Kenojuak, a triumph in graphic design.* [*National Gallery of Canada, Ottawa/Copyright West Baffin Eskimo Cooperative, Cape Dorset*]

1. *The town cemetery at Chesterfield Inlet, where lie buried explorers and Inuit alike.* [*Photo/Ian Creery*] 2. *A stone inukshuk. Inuit build them to serve as guideposts on the trackless tundra. A large replica of one stands as a symbol of Inuit life in the main foyer of the Department of Indian and Northern Affairs in Hull, Quebec.* [*Photo/ Jerry Guiberson*]

Perhaps the most remarkable thing about the Inuit is how well known they are, although so few in number. For many years they have captured the imagination of anthropologists, writers and filmmakers. Inuit words like *kayak*, *igloo* and *anorak* have found their way into the English language. Inuit artists, printmakers and sculptors contribute substantially to Canadian culture, and their work is internationally appreciated at world fairs and exhibitions. Inuit

1.

2.

politicians were instrumental in securing the protection of aboriginal rights in Canada's new constitution. Inuit MPs have been elected to parliament since 1979, and there are two Inuit Senators.

It is hard to imagine what Canada would be like without the Inuit. They were among the first inhabitants of this land, and have lived here, generation after generation, for thousands of years. The Inuit have not yet won the fight to save their culture, but it is in the interest of all Canadians that they succeed.

1-5. Inuit art, dramatically simple, highly treasured and very collectible: 1. "Whaling in Cumberland Sound, 1930s" (1977) by Tommy Novakeel, Pangnirtung Cooperative; 2. "Our Massive Friend" (1984) by Pudlo Pudlat, Copyright West Baffin Eskimo Cooperative, Cape Dorset; 3. "High Kick" (1984) by Agnes Nanogak, Holman Island Cooperative; 4. "Woman and Child with Kudlik" (1977) by Matthew Aqiggaaq, Sannavik Cooperative, Baker Lake; 5. A wallhanging embroidery with hunting scene and igloo by Seeloo of Eskimo Point. [Dept. of Indian and Northern Affairs]

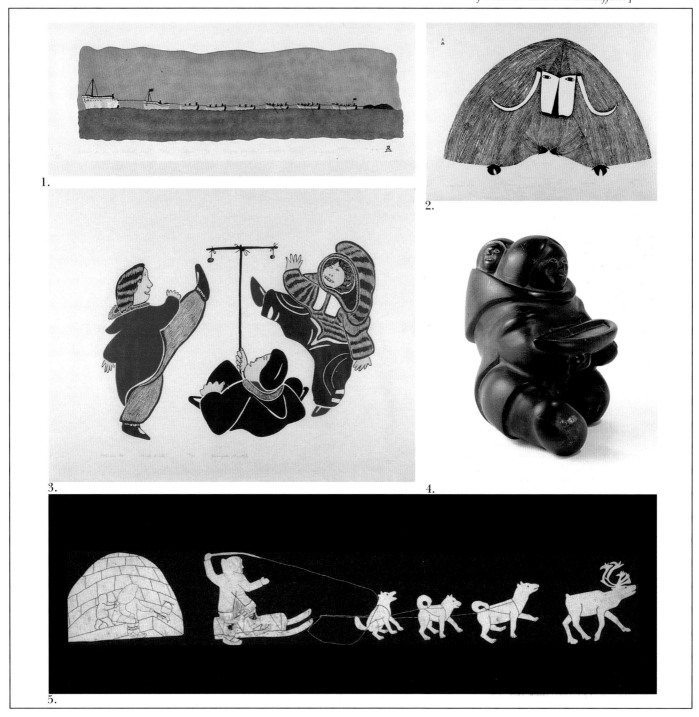

1.

2.

3.

4.

5.

Stamp: *The Metis were the descendants of Indian women who had married fur traders coming, for the most part, from their Montreal based headquarters. Louis Riel was an important leader of the Metis, and Indians, from the 1860s until 1885 when he was hanged for treason by the Government of Canada. The Canada Post Corporation commemorated Louis Riel, the founder of Manitoba, with this stamp in 1970.*

The Metis
by Antoine Lussier

PART I

In 1670, Charles II of England granted to the Hudson's Bay Company a fur trading monopoly in the area that today constitutes much of western Canada. Little was known about this hinterland except that furs were plentiful; very little was known, moreover, about the native peoples living in this great expanse.

During this period of time, a policy of economic assimilation was applied by the Hudson's Bay Company to this vast area destined to give birth to the Metis people upon the arrival of the European. People of mixed blood, the Metis chose to live neither the Indian's nor the white man's way of life. By the early 19th century, they had developed strong feelings of nationalism and group identity. This was the beginning of the Metis nation.

The concept of Metis nationalism is a western Canadian phenomenon. Unlike eastern Canada where church and state worked together in the hope of socially assimilating Indians, western Canada's native peoples were used for economic purposes. Since the Hudson's Bay

1. *"Wigwam", an Ojibway half-breed, 1858, with buffalo robe in background.* [*Metro Toronto Library [MTL]*] 2. *Letitia, a Cree half-breed, 1858.* [*MTL*] 3. *Mixed-blood women in tartan shawl — a typical wear for several generations, ca. 1907.* [*Glenbow Museum [GM]/NA-726-21*] 4. *John McKay, a Cree half-breed, 1858.* [*MTL*]

Company had fur trading forts along most rivers in this region, its purpose was better served by using the Indian for financial success. Dr. George Stanley, one of Canada's most respected historians today, has suggested that Indian squaws provided valuable contacts with Indians who had furs to dispose of.

Since mixed marriages were conducted *à la mode du pays*, it was easy for a fur trader to leave one native wife for a new one after being transferred to another area of the territory, sometimes hundreds of miles away.

Although Hudson's Bay Company partners in England condemned such marriage practices, they could not prevent them. Marriages to Indian women became trading necessities and no local governor would condemn the practice, especially since some were guilty of such relationships, including George Simpson, Governor at Lower Fort Garry.

The result of these marriages was obvious. Soon a population of Euro-Indians surrounded the fur trading posts. Because they often married within their own group, it was not long before they became a force. There were, of course, two types of Metis: the Anglo-Indian and the Franco-Indian. These people were closely knit, bound by a common Indian origin, their economic means of survival (the fur trade), and their western homeland. Not until they felt infringement upon their way of life did they form a strong nationalist movement. This came about with the forming of the first European colony in Western Canada.

In 1811, the Hudson's Bay Company granted 116,000 square miles of land in the Red River Valley to Lord Selkirk, hoping to establish both a permanent settlement and an agricultural economy in Western Canada. At the time, however, this company overlooked one factor—the nomadic Metis, caught in the middle between the Hudson's Bay Company and its arch rival, the North West Company. Since their loyalty leaned towards the Nor' Westers, it was predictable that the Metis would look unfavourably upon Lord Selkirk's mandate to settle the area. In fact, the Company's action was seen not only as a blatant attempt to destroy the North West Company, but as a concerted effort to impose an agricultural life upon a nomadic people. These facts gave rise to the birth of Metis nationalism and their goal of self-preservation!

PART II

The Metis led a simple life close to nature. Bishop Taché, who lived at Red River, wrote an account of his impressions of the Metis, describing their physical characteristics as handsome, large, strong and well-made. He lists a number of other traits: their powers of

2.

1. *Sir George Simpson (ca. 1787-1860), Governor of the Hudson's Bay Company in Canada, 1821-60. [Public Archives of Canada [PAC]]* 2. *Selkirk, Thomas Douglas, Fifth Earl of (1771-1820). Received in 1812 from the Hudson's Bay Company a large land grant called The Red River Colony. [PAC]*

1.

2.

1. *Archbishop Alexandre-Antoin Taché (1823-1894), missionary, Catholic priest at St. Boniface, Manitoba. [PAC] 2. Fifth Church (fourth cathedral) of St. Boniface. It burned to the ground in 1968. The facade stands today and nearby is the grave of Louis Riel.*

observation, excellent memory, sense of humour, intelligence and skill as horsemen. In a remarkable list of their virtues and faults, he includes under the former heading, their warm-heartedness, willingness to help, love for children, and their patience and honesty ("theft is a crime scarcely, if at all, known amongst Half-breeds").

Dedicated as they were to their church and their superiors, the Metis stressed the importance of their roles as husbands and wives. A Metis family was one characterized by affection and understanding. Authority lay in the hands of the father. It should be noted that Metis families were usually large.

The role of the Metis women was unique. They were often found with their respective husbands during the hunt, their responsibilities actually vital to the success of the hunt in that they followed with carts, taking the carcasses and converting them into pemmican.

It was also the duty of the Metis women to educate their children in the Roman Catholic religion. The influence of the church has always been vital for the Metis who, in their hunting expeditions, have traditionally kept the best meat for the priest. That the Metis respected the church and its teachings is reinforced in S.J. Dawson's *General Report on the Progress of the Red River Expedition* (1859). His writings state that he "never once heard an oath or an indelicate expression made use of among them."

In the community, Metis people were not different from the whites. They went about their tasks of farming or building new houses and sheds, attended church and lived as any other civilized person. They were very hospitable and did not think twice before sharing whatever they had with their guests.

These are the same people who rose to fight for their rights in 1816, 1849, 1870 and finally in 1885.

It was the Metis who, upon securing an identity which led them to regard themselves, with confidence, as a unique race in Western Canada, finally resisted the Canadian government in 1870, in turn, bringing about the premature entry of Manitoba into Confederation.

PART III

Violence began with the arrival of Lord Selkirk and his settlers in 1811-12. The bitter rivalry which had gone on between the Hudson's Bay Company (1670) and the North West Company (1784) reached a climax in 1812. It became obvious to the North West Company that Selkirk's grant meant the end of the fur trade. It also meant another means of existence—agriculture.

When Miles Macdonell, the first governor of the Red River Colony, proclaimed an embargo on the sale of pemmican, the North West Company had no choice but to force the Hudson's Bay colony to leave, obtaining, at the same time, Metis support. Stanley argues:

"At the door of the North West Company must be laid the responsibility for rousing the racial consciousness of the Metis. The Nor' Westers carefully fostered the idea of half-breed territorial rights and convinced the credulous Metis that the white settlers were interlopers who had come to steal the land from them."

Although the Metis had never really felt any hostility toward the Selkirk settlers, it did not take much for them to be aroused. The North West Company knew how to play upon the Metis and persuaded them that Indian origin meant title to the land and that Metis' freedoms would be taken. Thus, the North West Company was able to present a case for the Metis cause. Macdonell's proclamation prohibiting the exportation of pemmican and forbidding the Metis to run buffalo led to active aggression. In 1814-15, led by Duncan Cameron, among others, they began harassing Fort Douglas.

Macdonell surrendered, the fort was burnt to the ground, and crops trampled. After the new governor, Robert Semple, arrived, he not only died in battle but indirectly caused the eventual downfall of the North West Company. The 1816 episode in which Semple and 20 of his men died is called today by some historians, "the Massacre of Seven Oaks."

With the defeat of the North West Company, the two rival companies merged in 1821, leaving the Metis to themselves. The patriotic idea, however, of being Metis, the idea of national identity, persisted.

1.

1. *Miles Macdonell (ca. 1769-1828) first Governor of the Red River Colony. [Hudson's Bay Company]* 2. *The Fight at Seven Oaks, 1816, by C.W. Jefferys. [PAC/C-73663]* 3. *Cuthbert Grant (ca. 1793-1854), son of a North West Company employee and a Cree mother, led the Metis at Seven Oaks, June, 1816. [Manitoba Archives [MA]]*

2.

3.

Since further settlement was practically nil following the merger, it was inevitable that intermarriage within the Metis group took place. Gradually the European stock no longer constituted a threat to the Metis. Nevertheless, the Hudson's Bay Company still ruled. To the Metis, this represented an infringement upon their democratic rights.

The Metis always looked upon democracy as a government formed by the consent of the governed. In the 1820s, this concept of democracy was not in operation in Manitoba. The Hudson's Bay Company's governor represented authoritarianism to the Metis and could unequivocally overrule the council of Assiniboia. It was not until 1849 that the Metis at Red River finally broke the trade monopoly of the Hudson's Bay Company by forcing the Recorder's court to acquit Guillaume Sayer, a Metis, on charges of breach of Company regulations. This action marked the second time that the Metis had risen to the occasion. The Company would no longer attempt to impose its monopoly on the Metis community.

Up to this time, Red River had been an isolated post, somewhere in a forgotten world. Suddenly there was a growing interest in the Northwest. The ideal of land, wealth and fortune in northwestern America, or Rupert's Land, began to be the talk of ordinary citizens and governments in both Canada and the United States.

During the 1850s and 1860s, Red River's isolation from the Canadas and the United States slowly diminished. Communication was by way of Hudson Bay or through Minnesota. The result was an influx of people from the Canadas and the United States in search of new lands and wealth. Perhaps the most startling aspect of all was the constant cry for annexation either to the Canadas or to the United States. The more vocal group within the settlement was from Canada West, the future Ontario.

1. *An Advertisement for Saskatchewan Buffalo Robes, 1885. [John Young]* 2. *The Gathering of Buffalo Bones on the Alberta Prairie, ca. 1900. [C.J. Humber]*

1.

2.

In 1859, the first newspaper in the Canadian west, the *Nor' Wester*, was established in Red River by William Buckingham and William Coldwell. The paper was soon taken over by Dr. John Christian Schultz, leader of the Canadian party, a small but noisy group demanding annexation to Canada. Repudiating the role of the Hudsons's Bay Company as a form of government, the *Nor' Wester* roused Metis fears. It became apparent that something had to be done.

Thus in 1869, the Hudson's Bay Company sold the vast territory from the Red River to the Rockies for 300,000 pounds (sterling) to the Canadian government. The transfer date had been set for December 1, 1869. However, it was not to be. John A. Macdonald's hope of a nation "from sea unto sea" would have to wait a few more months. Negotiations, which had been proceeding since 1857, were held among three governments—The British, The Hudson's Bay Company and the Canadian. Not once were the people of the northwest ever consulted. They were neither informed about the proceedings, nor was anything explained to them. Small wonder, then, that the Metis reacted so negatively towards William McDougall, the governor designate, when he arrived at St. Norbert in October, 1869.

Of all the groups that formed the Red River settlement, only the Canadians favoured union. Company employees, the Metis, clergy,

1. *September 7, 1869 edition of the* Nor'Wester. [*MA*] *2. The West's first newspaper, the* Nor'Wester, *was published in Winnipeg, 1859.* [*MA*] *3. Dr. John Christian Schultz (1840-1896), Owner of the* Nor'Wester, Attacked the "Tyranny" *of the Hudson's Bay Company, and Demanded the Annexation of the Red River Colony to Canada.* [*PAC*]

1.

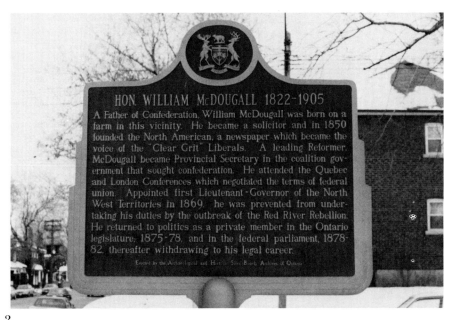

2.

1. *William McDougall (1822-1905). As a Member of Parliament, he introduced a resolution that led to the puchase of Rupert's Land.* 2. *A plaque erected near the corner of Yonge St. and Lawrence Ave. in Toronto in honour of William Mc-Dougall (1822-1905), a Father of Confeder-ation.* [*C.J. Humber*] 3. *Thomas Scott (ca. 1842-1870). His execution led to armed intervention by the Canadian government during the Red River crisis of 1870.* [*PAC/ C-25589*]

3.

old Selkirk settlers and, of course, the Americans, looked upon it with reservations. Furthermore, few people within the settlement really understood the events that were taking place. As they began to realize the implications of union, the Metis people took action. Under the firm leadership of Louis Riel Jr., the Metis resisted, using the concepts of international law as their base. A government *ex necessitate* was established. This government, though not recognized by Ottawa, was clearly the body speaking for the people of Red River, and Macdonald sent delegates to negotiate with it.

It was this provisional government that set up the List of Rights and fought for Manitoba's entry into Confederation as a province and not a territory (as had at first been suggested).

However, Metis' efforts never went without some degree of resistance. Throughout the proceedings, the Canadian party continued to harass the provisional government and attempted twice to overthrow it. Although their attempts failed, arrests were inevitable. It was because of the arrest of one man, who was later executed, that the Metis nation began to decline.

Thomas Scott, a Protestant from Ontario, was working as a labourer in the Red River settlement. He became involved in the Canadian party's attempt to overthrow the provisional government and was arrested and executed. Scott's execution made him a martyr of the Canadian party's cause and led to armed intervention by the Canadian government in the Red River settlement.

The Metis fought on. Not until Manitoba's entry into Confederation as a province with all provincial rights in 1870 did the Metis succumb to pressure. That pressure was to come with the arrival of Colonel Wolseley and his troops who were sent from Canada by Macdonald to restore "order".

STANDING ORDERS

FOR THE

RED RIVER EXPEDITIONARY FORCE.

TORONTO, 14th May, 1870.

1. The Expeditionary Force will proceed from the end of the Thunder Bay Road to the Lake of the Woods in boats. It will move by Detachments, consisting of one or more Companies. To each Company a Brigade of 5 boats will be attached.

1.

35. All Officers belonging to this Force will be most careful in impressing upon those under their command the great necessity there is for cultivating the good will of the Indians and others employed as voyageurs.

Colonel Wolseley will punish with the utmost severity any one who ill treats them.

The same rule applies to all Indians who may be met on the line of route.

It must be remembered that the Government has made a treaty with them securing the right of way through their country; all are therefore bound to protect them from injury, and it is of special importance that our intercourse with them should be of the most friendly nature.

No Indians but those actually attached to the Force are to be allowed to pass the night in our Camps.

(Signed,) G. J. WOLSELEY,
Colonel Commanding Expeditionary Force.

3.

2.

1. *The Initial Clause of the Standing Orders of the "Red River Expeditionary Force".* [*John Young*] 2. *Colonel G.J. Wolseley (1833-1913) was sent to Manitoba by Sir John A. Macdonald to restore "order" after the first Riel uprising in 1870.* [*PAC*] 3. *The Final Clause of the Standing Orders Signed by Colonel Wolseley, 1870.* [*John Young*] 4. *A Telegram Sent Home by G.S. Ryerson, April 1, 1885, While on his Way to Quell the North-West Rebellion of 1885.* [*John Young*]

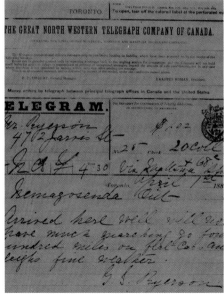

4.

PART IV

Upon their arrival, Wolseley's troops set out to find the "traitor" Louis Riel. However, he had fled the country along with some of his compatriots. Frustrated by their inability to find the villain, Wolseley's men began to ransack Metis' homes.

During the period of Wolseley's stay in Manitoba there was bloodshed. Though Governor Archibald had arrived, he could not control the volunteers who went about brawling. On at least one occasion this brawling ended in the unpunished killing of Elzear Goulet, a Metis. Such actions were not uncommon until Wolseley's expedition left to go back to Ontario.

With the passing of the Manitoba Act in 1870, everything seemed to have gone according to plan, everything, that is, except two important details, one of which was part of the Act. The first was

1.

2.

1. *Sir Frederick D. Middleton (1825-1898), Efficient Commander of Canadian Militia which Overcame Reil's 1885 Rebellion. [John Young]* 2. *General William D. Otter (1843-1929), One of the Commanders Repelling the Riel Rebellion of 1885. [John Young]* 3. *A Poster Advertising Half-breed Lands in Manitoba, 1876. [John Young]*

OPPOSITE Louis Riel (1844-1885), the Metis leader who founded Manitoba and was hanged for treason in 1885. [PAC/ C-121142]

the amnesty to be granted Riel. Under pressure from Ontario, Riel became a man without a country. Thrice elected to the House of Commons, he could not sit because of the price upon his head.

The second perhaps more important detail was the question of land. Prime Minister Macdonald would not grant the new province the right to control its resources. Neither would his government grant the new province the right to control public lands. He was determined to see that the Federal government controlled this matter. This meant that settlement in the west would strictly come under Federal jurisdiction. The Metis were to be given 1,400,000 acres of land, extinguishing their aboriginal title. Whether the total was actually received by them is no longer debatable. Recent evi-

3.

dence has shown it was not. What is most surprising is that the land was not given to the heads of Metis families, but to the children. W.L. Morton states that it was only after 1877 that Metis parents were eligible to receive land. Small wonder that shortly after 1870 many Metis people sought to leave the area.

Persecuted and discriminated against, they sought new land where they could continue their way of life. Their faith in the new government of Canada further diminished when John A. Macdonald described the land schemes as being more important than "the protests of 10,000 half-castes." Many Metis lost their land—some practically gave it away while others were swindled out of it.

After 1870, the Metis population was divided into three groups: (a) those who remained and identified with the Indians, joining them under the reserve system; (b) those who worked on farms and were assimilated into the white culture; and (c) a third group consisting of wanderers attempting to live the old life of fur trading. Following the buffalo along the plains, they settled in North Dakota and Montana. Later, driven out by American colonization, they came back to Canada and settled along the North Saskatchewan River, where in 1885 the Metis sought to make one last stand against the Canadian government. Once again they were led by Louis Riel only to have their dreams and aspirations shattered by the advancement of Canadian expansionism.

1. *Debates in the House of Commons were lively after the execution of Louis Riel.* [*John Young*] 2. *Louis Riel's Council, 1885, after their leader's arrest.* [*MA*]

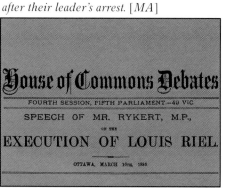

1.

2.

2.

1.

3.

PART V

Historically the term Metis was used to identify, predominantly, the Roman Catholic French speaking mixed bloods. Today the term is used to identify anyone with Indian blood who is not an Indian by law or a self-proclaimed non-status Indian. No longer is history, tradition or heritage used as the measures for identity. Indian ancestry is now the norm. Because of this, the social and economic issues among the Metis have been relegated to second place in the face of the political debate. Western Canadian Metis Organizations argue the historical basis for identity while the National Organization argues for Indian ancestry. Thus the priority placed on identity has overtaken the need for attention to the social and economic issues which concern the Metis people.

1. *Poundmaker (1842-1886), ca. 1875, a Cree Supporter of Louis Riel during the 1885 Rebellion. [PAC]* 2. *Metis Gabriel Dumont (1837-1906), a guerrilla leader, fought vigorously for Metis rights in the 1885 North-West Rebellion. [PAC/C-27663]* 3. *Riel, Manitoba is the cancellation mark on this commemorative stamp in 1937. [John Young]*

The Monumental Cultures of the Northwest Coast Peoples
Joan Ryan and Carol Sheehan

Stamp: *A Canada Post Corporation Stamp Illustrating a Northwest Coast chief with Chilkat Blanket and Ceremonial Headdress. Standing in the Background are cedar "monuments".*

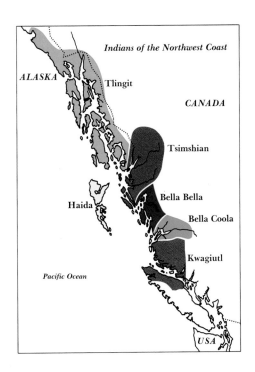

The people of the Northwest Coast cultures are hunting and gathering groups who have developed one of the richest and most distinctive lifestyles in human history. Masters of their maritime environment, they have five separate language stocks, and eight principal groupings or "tribes" who share an essentially similar culture. Ranging from north to south, they are the Tlingit of southeastern Alaska, the Haida of the Prince of Wales Archipelago and the Queen Charlotte Islands, the Tsimshian of the Nass and Skeena Rivers, the Northern and Southern Kwagiutl from Milbanke Sound to Rivers Inlet and the east coast of Vancouver Island, the Bella Coola from the upper reaches of Dean and Burke Channels, the Nootkan or Nuu-chah-nulth of the west coast of Vancouver Island, and the Coast Salish of the Straits of Georgia from Campbell River to Puget Sound.

"The guests are arriving! The guests are arriving!" The call goes out to all the bighouses. Chiefs and their families come out to stand in front of their houses, flanked by massive welcome figures and totem poles carved from the mighty cedars. Dressed in full regalia, they await their guests whom they will honour with a monumental feast. "The guests are arriving!"

The pageantry begins as the long graceful canoes of the guests come into the protected cove. The sight of rows of oarsmen pulling against the paddles of their longboats in graceful unison is impressive. Their song is deep and powerful. Each guest, rightly honoured by the invitation, is there to witness and honour the public proclamation of the hosts' claims to property and status. All the people are dressed in their finest and most prestigious regalia. Ermine, woven mountain goat wool, painted wood and hide, abalone, flicker feathers and eagle down glisten in the royal robes of the crowd waiting on the beach.

The village chiefs walk toward the shore where they greet the arriving chiefs with formal speeches and cordiality. Ranked nobility and commoners interact with visible deference to guests and to each other. These are important moments establishing alliances which will ensure shared resources, help in times of war, and the endurance of clans, crests and families. Events must be carried out carefully and with considerable courtesy; to insult a guest is to insult a nation, to breach alliances. Guests today are hosts tomorrow.

This scene, enacted thousands of times in the magnificent rain

1.

1. *Tsimshian Chiefs in Ceremonial Dress, ca 1920.* [*C.J. Humber*] 2. *First Chief Skadeem of Gitlakdamiks, Photo/Marius Barbeau, ca 1920.* [*British Columbia Provincial Museum* [*BCPM*]/*PN4193*] 3. *"Coming of the Bride", photo/E.S. Curtis, 1914.* [*Library of Congress* [*LC*]/*U5262-52200*] 4. *Haida Artists, Tom Rice and John Robson, in Ceremonial Attire, Wearing Headdress of high-rank.* [*BCPM/PN5304*] 5. *"The Guests are Arriving", ca. 1860.* [*Glenbow Archives* [*GA*]/*NA-1807-57*] 6. *"Hosts Welcoming Guests", ca. 1900.* [*BCPM/PN9197*]

4.

3.

5.

6.

forests of the Northwest Coast, brings to mind again and again the concept of "monumentality" which describes the sights and sounds of the Northwest Coast. With the vast array of cultural properties and themes found there, it is artificial to develop a single concept with which to view a people and a way of life. Nonetheless, used as a key concept for illuminating the objects, events and ideas of this remarkable coastal environment, a theme such as monumentality is a useful explanatory tool that gives interesting glimpses into these unique and complex cultures.

Dugout cedar canoes, like the ones approaching the beach, were the main mode of transportation on the coast and here too is a case for monumental proportion and effort. Moving from a winter village site to the summer one was often facilitated by lashing several large canoes together, catamaran style, with cedar house planks. This rafting technique also provided a floating stage for the dancers from one village to make a spectacular water arrival at the feast site of their neighbours.

Masters of the sea, the Northwest Coast people set standards for endurance and distance with these vessels. The Haida routinely travelled the inside passage in summer from their homeland on the Queen Charlotte Islands to Victoria Harbour — over 600 miles away. The Nuu-chah-nulth ventured into unpredictable and fierce Pacific waters to hunt the mammoth grey whales — a monumental task in an open dugout canoe, the hunter armed with only bone-tipped harpoons.

The various lifestyles of the Northwest Coast people are rich in relationships, accommodating the living and the dead and include belief systems which direct socialization, and political and economic development. Children are born into large extended families. Summers have always been spent fishing, collecting, drying, and now canning and freezing fish. In the fall, hunting and gathering continue and the winters are still partially spent in the traditional ways: feasting and gathering together for spiritual events.

In order to host the monumental feasts, extended families require access to considerable resource wealth. Such wealth derives from the ability of family heads to command the human and environmental resources to accumulate, process and store foods. In more recent times, there is a cash flow which permits the hosts to feed hundreds of people, to give away food and to present gifts of art, blankets, furnishings, jewelry, and the like. As has always been the case, gallons of the pungent *oolachen* or candle fish oil, highly prized and very expensive, are given as prestigious gifts. Such generosity requires the labour of many people and a system of indebtedness allows one to call in debts and thus to acquire the

OPPOSITE: An Abandoned Nuu-chah-nulth Canoe, 16.7 Metres Long, Photographed at Clo-ose, Vancouver Island, 1912. Carved from the monumental trunk of a single western cedar, this superb example of native technology, and one of the largest "dugout" canoes recorded, has vanished without a trace. [Carol Sheehan]

labour and resources needed to meet the responsibilities of the hosts.

The ritual system is a viable economic and political one which allows the debtor to collect payments on subsequent occasions. Only an abundant resource base such as the Northwest Coast provides could allow this kind of system to operate well and in full balance. In the past, there were misunderstandings between natives and non-natives that were prompted by the ostentatious displays at feasts and potlatches; these led to the outlawing of gatherings by the Canadian government. At one time, the imposition of these laws was enforced by some missionaries and the RCMP. This led to the deterioration of the festivals, but not to their extinction. Some went underground, some evolved in different forms, some continued, and some were lost. When the misguided law was removed in 1951, a major job of revitalization and adaptation faced the peoples of the Northwest Coast.

1. *Kwagiutl Potlatch Gifts Displayed in Front of the Big Houses in Alert Bay. [C.J. Humber]* 2. *Kwagiutl Crest Pole in Front of a Ceremonial House. Potlatch gifts of blankets are stacked beside the pole. The images on the pole are, from top to bottom: Sun and Thunderbird, Killer Whale, Chief holding a copper, and Grizzly Bear biting a copper. [C.J. Humber]*

1.   2.

The spiritual ambience that continues to fuel these efforts also has its place in the realm of the monumental. Natural and super-natural worlds are contiguous in Northwest Coast cultures — the powers in both are the subject of a broad body of beliefs and practices. The peoples of the Northwest Coast developed complex rituals and systems of explanation which are given their fullest and most graphic portrayal in the music, dances, story-telling and paraphernalia of the winter ceremonials. These events are expressions made by people who are very much in tune with the seasonal and cosmological cycles that affects the universe and their place within it. Again, we see the making of larger-than-life statements — monumental expressions — that serve their creators well in making supernatural and social worlds not only visible, but manageable.

In the north, family and clan identities are proudly displayed in the form of crests, the symbolic emblems that visually mark everything from canoe prows to clothing, from masks to halibut

Chilkat Blanket or "Dancing Blanket" worn by High Ranking Men and Women of the Northern Northwest Coast. This ceremonial garment was woven on a vertical loom with a warp of twined mountain goat wool and the inner bark of the yellow cedar tree. The weft threads were pure dyed mountain goat wool. [Carol Sheehan]

hooks, from carved feast dishes to painted house fronts. The crests usually have zoomorphic forms, though botanical and celestial motifs are sometimes used as well. In the south, family names and symbols identify extended families and important people. The images are not worshipped; rather they visually and symbolically portray a family's history and prerogatives that may be traced to prehistoric times — to the myth times.

Monumentality is an easy concept with which to view the huge cedar houses, canoes and totem poles of the Northwest Coast cultures

1.

1. *Many of the Northwest Coast Indian villages stand today as monuments to a culture eroded by the encroaching civilization of the white man. This picture of Skidegate, on the east coast of Queen Charlotte Islands, was taken in 1878 by explorer George Dawson. [Geological Survey of Canada, Ottawa]* 2. *Southern Kwagiutl House Posts Representing Sea Lions Holding in Their Mouths a Carved Double-headed Serpent. This monumental house frame is shown on its original setting in Quatsino Sound at the Koskimo village of Quattishe. The house posts have been removed to the University of British Columbia Museum of Anthropology. [Carol Sheehan]*

2.

for they are the most obvious and stunning visual features of these woodworking peoples. Physically, these objects are tremendous engineering feats. The houses were constructed from large planks taken from the clean and true-splitting red cedar. The massive corner posts, gable and roof beams were often several feet in diameter. The bighouses of the coast ranged from 30-40 feet in width by 60-80 feet in depth, and housed several families and their slaves in the times of traditional living.

The houses were built of larger and sturdier materials than they needed to be; the size of the logs and planks was far greater than was required for structural stability and strength. Perhaps the reason for the building of this kind of monumental structure is ensconced in the cultural idea that in addition to being a residence for people and families, the house became a symbolic and metaphorical cosmos in the winter ceremonies. It was a centre of the universe that was inhabited by not only mere mortals, but by supernatural actors as well.

Houses, both traditional and modern, continue to be the setting for the sacred and secular events of the winter ceremonials. People come to these feasts, potlatches and spirit dances for different reasons. One occasion might be a marriage, linking different clans and tribal groups to broader resource bases — and therefore to greater wealth. Such unions are carefully considered and people are expected to marry the right people. Perhaps the gathering is called in memory of a person deceased years ago but still present in name and property. Frequently, such an occasion is accompanied by other important events: the formalities of witnessing the passing of names or property, the initiation of a crest dancer, the first naming of a child, and the celebration of the completion of the puberty rites.

It is during the winter that the most elaborate feasts, displays, "the big times", namings, and initiations reassert one's place in the group and one's full responsibility to it. Whatever the event, people attend to listen to the many speeches, to witness the public proclamations, to display family dances and to have their lives transformed from the mundane to the spectacular. It is on this firelit stage, a centre of the universe, that masks are worn, elaborate dramas are unfolded and power-full songs are danced. Mere mortals are transformed into supernatural spirits — and back again. The community is transformed, enriched and reaffirmed through the enactment of what may be termed "rituals of rightness" that serve to link human experience with the rest of the cosmos.

There are other linkages too. The deceased are gone in body only. Their presence is still active in the communities; people still

"The Inside of a House in Nootka Sound"
This engraving from A New, Authentic, and Complete Collection of Voyages Around the World of Capt. Cook *(1784) suggests that the day-to-day living of the Northwest Coast Indians was remarkably "monu-mental". [Public Archives of Canada/C-3676]*

1.

2.

3.

1. *Kwagiutl Ceremonial Cress Headdress Representing a Killer Whale and an Eagle or Thunderbird. [Glenbow Museum Collection [GMC]/AA-1746]* **2.** *Headdress, ceremonial, Bear Design, Probably Kwagiutl. The eyes, nostrils and teeth are of abalone shell. Sea lion whiskers rise vertically. [GMC/AA-1682 A & B]* **3.** *Coast Salish Swaixwe Mask. Still used today, this kind of mask is featured in purification ceremonies and winter spirit dances. [GMC/ R-5122]*

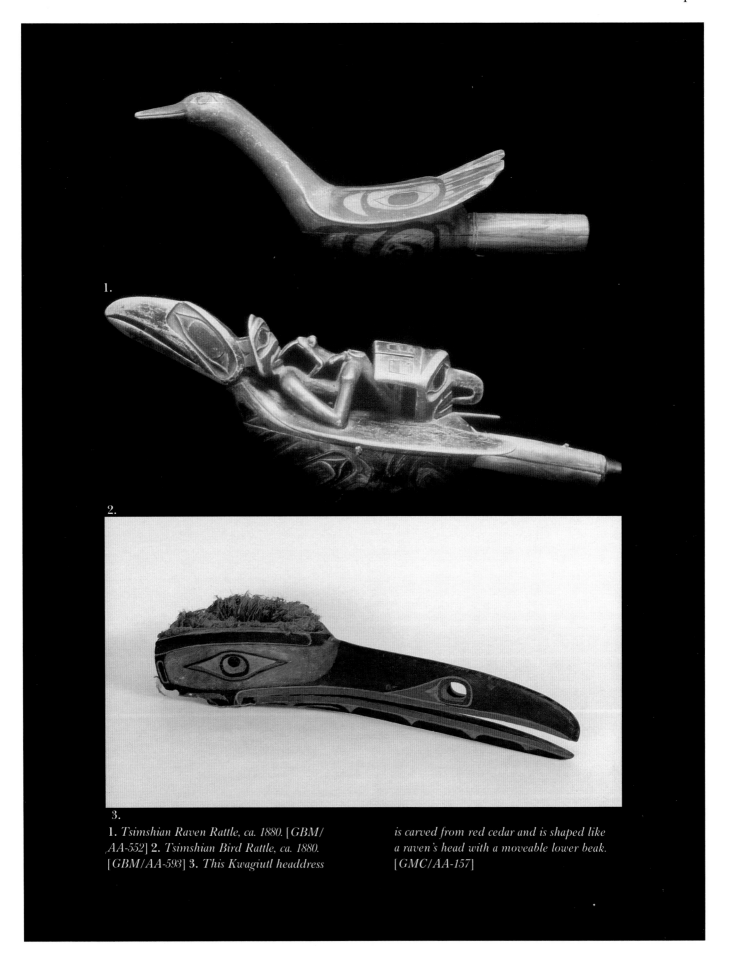

1.

2.

3.

1. *Tsimshian Raven Rattle, ca. 1880.* [*GBM/ AA-552*] 2. *Tsimshian Bird Rattle, ca. 1880.* [*GBM/AA-593*] 3. *This Kwagiutl headdress* *is carved from red cedar and is shaped like a raven's head with a moveable lower beak.* [*GMC/AA-157*]

1.

1. Kwagiutl Mortuary Monuments, Alert Bay, ca. 1910. [C.J. Humber] 2. Haida Argillite Sculpture, Bear Mother Tableau, ca. 1900. [GMC/AA-1987] 3. Haida Bear-Mother Sculpture in rare "red argillite". [GMC/AA-1885] 4. Haida Bear-Mother Sculpture. [GMC/AA-1988] 5. Contemporary Carving by Haida Artist Steve Collinson Depicting Bear-Mother Myth. [GMC]

consult them, and new progeny in the family are capable of becoming the reincarnated relatives. There is no break between the living and the dead; the continuity of generations is never severed. Similarly the relationship between human beings can be transformed by ritual means to alternative states. With these universal dynamics, ceremonial performances are carefully dramatized because failure to execute them properly could result in soul loss and cultural, if not physical, death.

Initiations of spirit dancers and masked dancers proceed, therefore, with full witness and protocol to ensure the safe passage of individuals through all stages of life and death. Such persons also achieve great stature and respect and become special people within the community. These monumental events attempt to synchronize a world, in balance, for both individuals and collectivities.

These events are statements of power and of the dynamics of power within various levels of human awareness and experience. Mythtime merges here with history; transformation ceremonies can change humans into supernatural beings and counterparts from other realms can assume human forms. Philosophy and belief are translated into action and become teachings for the novices, lessons for the initiated.

Contemporary peoples of the Northwest Coast continue their traditions in innovative and adaptive ways. Slavery no longer exists and it is commonplace for several families to co-host gatherings

2.

3.

4.

5.

sharing labour, natural and monetary resources. Marriages and divorces are primarily civic ceremonies now, but are still witnessed in contemporary bighouses. There are also important names and property to pass hands, and initiations to carry out. The combination of a cash and subsistence economy has compressed the time and extent of some gatherings, but the same gatherings have added the dimensions of guests arriving by jet and of being preserved on film, video and in the press. Nevertheless, the essence remains: people still receive names, get initiated, learn their family histories and dances, don their masks and blankets, and honour the living and the dead. They continue to gossip, to laugh and cry, to dance with all the power and vitality of the past brought into the present. Their endurance is monumental.

1. *Cedar Tree at Windy Bay on Lyell Island, Queen Charlotte Islands. This spectacular cedar tree bears the ancient marks of Haida women's cedar bark gathering. The soft inner bark fibers were harvested as the raw materials of basketry and weaving arts. Bark and whole planks were taken from the living cedar without destroying the tree.* [*Photo/Carol Sheehan*] 2. *Coast Salish Cradle or Baby Cradle, ca. 1890. Made from cedar tree fibers found along the Pacific Coast.* [*GMC/1824*]

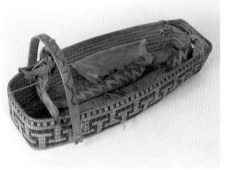

2.

1.

Index

Patrons

Without the generous support of corporate sponsors from across Canada, Heirloom Publishing Inc. would not have been able to create the *CANADA Heirloom Series*, in general, and Volume II of the series, *CANADA's Native Peoples*, in particular.

Additionally, *CANADA's Native Peoples* acknowledges the support of the *Government of Ontario*, through the Ministry of Culture and Communications, the Honourable Lily Munro, Minister.

The following list acknowledges these patrons:

ABC Group
Ace Computers
Alchem Inc.
All Canada Sports Promotions Ltd.
Allinson-Ross Corporation
Apple Canada Inc.
Armbro Enterprises Inc.
The Arrow Company
Arthur Andersen & Co.
Arvak Limited
Atlantis Group Inc.
Atomic Energy of Canada Ltd.
Babcock & Wilcox Canada
Bachan Aerospace of Canada Ltd.
G.E. Barbour Company Ltd.
Baton Broadcasting
Bic Inc.
Blue Cross of Canada
Bridgestone (Canada) Inc.
T.G. Bright & Co. Ltd.
Bristol Aerospace Limited
Cala H.R.C. Ltd.
Canadian Fracmaster Ltd.
Canadian National Exhibition Ass.
Canon Canada Inc.
Cantel Inc.
Cape Breton Development Corp.
Carrier Canada Limited
Central Guaranty Trustco
Chester Industrial Tool Supply
Chrysler Canada Ltd.
The Citadel Assurance
CN Marine
Cockshutt Greenhouses Ltd.
COM DEV Limited
Community Nursing Homes Ltd.
The Complax Corporation
Con-Drain Company Limited
Connor, Clark & Co. Ltd.
Consolidated Fastfrate Transport
Cuddy International Corp.
Curwood Packaging (Canada) Ltd.
CVL Inc.
Dean Witter (Canada) Inc.
Delta Hotels
Delta Electric Co. Ltd.
Dow Corning Canada Inc.
Drake International
Ducks Unlimited Canada
The Dufferin Group of Companies
Earl C. McDermid Limited

T. Eaton Company
Ed. Mirvish Enterprises
Fednav Limited
Fiberglas Canada Inc.
Filter Queen Limited
Financial Trustco Capital Ltd.
Fisher Gauge Limited
The Foundation Group
Four Seasons Drywall
The Four Seasons Hotels
Gelco Express Limited
General Motors of Canada
Gibbard Furniture Shops Ltd.
Golden Griddle Pancake Houses
Halliburton Services Ltd.
Hamilton Computer Sales & Rentals
Reg. Municipality of Hamilton-Wentworth
Hatch Associates
Hayes-Dana Filters Inc.
Henry Birks & Sons Ltd.
Hoover Canada Inc.
Imperial Lumber Co. Ltd.
Imperial Oil Limited
Inco Limited
Innopac Inc.
Dr. H.D.E. Inns Associates
Interconnect Equipment Systems
Intercontinental Packers Ltd.
Irene Hill Limited
The Irving Companies
Janssen Pharmaceutica Inc.
Johnson Controls
Knob Hill Farms
Knoch Manufacturing Company
Lawson Mardon Group Limited
LeBlanc & Royle Enterprises
MacDonald, Dettwiler & Associates
Magna International Inc.
The Manufacturers Life Insurance Company
Mary Kay Cosmetics Ltd.
McBee Technographics Inc.
McCain Foods Limited
McDonald's Restaurants of Canada
Melitta Canada Inc.
Molly Maid Home Care Services
Morton-Parker Limited
Molson Breweries of Canada Ltd.
The Montreal Canadiens
The Montreal Expos
Moore Corporation
MTM Inc.

National Bank of Canada
National Life of Canada
National Sea Products Ltd.
Noranda Forest Sales Inc.
Norman Wade Canada Ltd.
OEB International
Ogivar Inc.
Olympia & York Enterprises Inc.
Ontario Chrysler
Ontario Hydro
Osler Hoskin & Harcourt
Oxford Frozen Foods
Pannell Kerr MacGillivray
Paramax Electronics Inc.
Parkwood Chev, Olds, Cadillac
Pitney Bowes of Canada Ltd.
Pizza Delight
Power Corporation of Canada
Principal Group
Prudential Assurance
RCS-Netherwood
Reichhold Limited
Royal Bank of Canada
City of Saint John, N.B.
St. Joseph Printing
The Seagram Company Ltd.
Sears Canada Inc.
SED Systems
W.H. Smith Ltd.
Smitty's Pancake Houses Ltd.
Somerville Belkin Industries Ltd.
Southam Murray Printing
Spar Aerospace Ltd.
Springwall East
Stelco Inc.
Syncrude Canada Ltd.
Texas Instruments
W.G. Thompson & Sons Ltd.
Thomson (Canada) Rivet Co. Ltd.
Tiger Brand Knitting
Toronto Blue Jays Baseball Club
Toronto Stock Exchange
The Toronto Star
Triple E Canada Limited
Unilever Canada Limited
VS Services Ltd.
Wagner Signs Incorporated
Walbar of Canada
P.J. Ward Associates Ltd.
W.C. Wood Company Limited
The W.G. Young Co. Ltd.